73

Gentleman Practice

CஐB

a collection of work
by Buddy Wakefield

Write Bloody Publishing
America's Independent Press

Long Beach, CA

writebloody.com

Wakefield, Buddy.
2nd edition.
ISBN: 978-1-935904-10-6

Interior Layout by Lea C. Deschenes
Cover Design by Chris A'lurede
Cover Layout by David Ayllon
Proofread by Jennifer Roach
Edited by Cristin O'Keefe Aptowicz, Derrick Brown, Jaimie Garbacik, Timmy Straw and
    Courtney Olsen
Type set in Helvetica by Linotype and Bergamo: www.theleagueofmoveabletype.com

Also by Buddy Wakefield: *Live for a Living* and *Some They Can't Contain*

Special thanks to Lightning Bolt Donor, Weston Renoud

Printed in Tennessee, USA

Write Bloody Publishing
Long Beach, CA
Support Independent Presses
writebloody.com

To contact the author, send an email to writebloody@gmail.com

DEDICATION

This book is for people who keep thinking their work is done, people who've yet to break through the rest of the resistance, who aim to thrive but still get stuck in the excuse. Don't stop arriving. You're almost there. You know the clearing is just ahead. I know because we are happening at the same time.

This book is for people who keep showing up to support someone else unfolding, to bear witness to themselves, to see if something true of heart will happen.

GENTLEMAN PRACTICE

GENTLEMAN PRACTICE

THE BULLET POINTS

CONVERSATION WITH TODD SICKAFOOSE

BUDDY: I don't wanna be like the lady in *Radical Acceptance* who wakes up from a coma on her death bed and realizes what a waste it was that she spent her entire life worrying something was wrong with her. I'd like to know there's nothing wrong with me.

TODD: Or that it's okay if something is.

ABOUT THE AUDIENCE

In the dream I was onstage and there were thousands of you goin' bananas for me, all laughing and clapping, celebrating your brains out, not because I was somethin' else up there, but because you were just so happy I was finally starting to get it.

ABOUT GETTING IT

In the dream, I was using a square shovel to remove blubber crud from an oval tub. I know it was called blubber crud because my dream said so. It can be somewhat difficult to shovel crud from an oval tub with a square shovel. I was having a rough time of it. Then the voice of reason showed up and said, "Hey, Bud . . . this is *your* dream."

So I shape-shifted the square shovel into an oval shovel and began shoveling again, quite efficiently at that. The new oval shovel fit perfectly into the oval ends of the tub. It was an easier job for sure. I worked and worked and worked. Then the voice of reason came back to me and said, "Buddy, listen ... this is *your dream.*"

So I disappeared the tub and I stopped shoveling shit and I woke up.

BIBLIOGRAPHY

This is a nonfiction account of a relay race to the light.
I don't claim to be properly cross-referenced beyond the self-indulgence or noble aspirations, but I have a good feeling I'm on the right track.
I am still very much unfolding from a memory of ransacked truths.
Openly human.
Stunt water.
I can fit any word into my mouth and speak it clearly.
At some point I have eaten most of them.

INTENTION

To stand firm in the presence of God so that I consistently choose right action (assuming *firm = clarity and compassion, God = all that is,* and *right action* leads to *real happiness*).

EDIT

*Jordan tattoos the words **FORGIVE ME***
in thick black letters down the inside of his arm,
so that when he looks at his wrist
he will remember to not hate himself so much.

That's from a poem called "Human the Death Dance."
I've since seen folks with **FORGIVE ME** tattoos down the inside of their arms.

We'd probably both feel better about it if you'd go ahead and add an "N" to the word **FORGIVE** just as soon as you're able.

THE RESIST ANTS
(1995)

Little boys talk all day
about the mistakes they've made,
say they cannot do anything
without getting lost in it,

so they dance in a stitch of wit
to defend but not use their gifts,
and they can dance while they hold their breath,
but it don't mean they're proud of it—

how they've all got God's attention,
and how they've all come all this way,
and how they all wanna make a statement,
but they're not sure what to say.

Not one knows what to say.

HOME

Remember when you were four years old
and your room looked like a war zone,
so Mom insisted you would be doing nothing with the rest of your life
until it was clean;
every last puzzle piece, every toy part, every game component,
all the action figures and clothes,
replace the stuffies,
make the bed,
including the top bunk,
which is a bitch for four-year-olds,
remember?
You took one look and said
"No,"
then threatened to run away.

So Mom helped you pack —

got ya all bundled and zipped up
for the dead of winter
in that same puffy jacket most of us poor kids had,
the one that looked like navy blue tires stacked on top of each other.
Remember? She tucked a scratchy yarn scarf 'round yer neck,
the one MeMaw made,
the one you were allergic to,
handed you a scary anecdote about killer hitchhikers
scooted ya on out the front door,
then shut the door,
and locked it.
Remember how fired up you got,
them huffy red cheeks
ready to speak your piece
in the name of everything dinnerlessed and unfaired.
You were gonna tell her a thing or two
just before she calmly closed the blinds in your face.
'Member that?
And remember each weighted pause
as you heavy-stepped it down the frozen front porch
cursing this wicked woman
who just so happened to make a fantastic macaroni and cheese?
But you stuck to your guns
and you ran away into the long cold winter

for ten minutes

to the edge of the driveway

where you realized

at four years old

there is no other destination than home.

I remember seeing your exhale blow back across the driveway.

Do you remember
how fast you ran for the house with all your heart

20

flailing that epiphany,
ready to reveal a changed mind,
how you crammed your whole life through the front door as they opened it,
rushed straight to the center of the living room,
shook off the snow and planted yourself,
looked everybody right in the eyes,
expecting some warm reunion when you told them
you had revised your choice
and that you would now in fact be cleaning up the war zone you'd created,
but how no one said anything except
Oh …
we thought you had run away?
Remember that?

That moment is responsible for my hate

and my sense of humor.

You can call me an angry ghost when I'm gone,
or you can laugh into my disposition,
but my mom will still see me
as her wide-eyed wanderer
out behind the garage
inventing ways to fend off dog attacks
that will probably never happen.
I picked the scabs from my knees
because Mom said it would leave a scar …

Awesome.

CONVERSATION WITH STEVEN ARROWOOD

BUDDY: Maybe I can't get as far with honesty.

STEVE: Guess it depends where you're going.

TAUGHT

In the third grade,
Coach Hendrix dumped a parachute onto the gymnasium floor
and had us spread it out flat
like a bed sheet
for windmills.

Whole class stood curious
all the way around the edge of it,
knelt down when he told us to
and gripped on with both hands tight.

Taut.

Not letting go
on the count of three,
we flung our arms above our heads
and ran into the middle.

Hear me when I tell you look up,
and a little at the way you're breathing,
colliding in the middle again.
Today it's not kickball and win.

Loose up.

A pocket of air is unfolding
from the way you're withholding love.
If you mean it to speak black hole like that
there will be no word for warmth.

Mean it to speak your form.
When the safety comes to greet us
you will know it did not come easy.
Go easy on this.

Explain nothing.

Hold still from retelling the tragedy.

Resistance quits colliding.
Good god resenting safety
has become unnecessary.

Dove teeth sunk in a parking lot.
Festival face in a blanket fort.
Floodlight lasting fastly.
A carnival held in a cup.

Coach Hendrix

watched me run into the red
with nearly every blackout.
All the endings gave me blackouts.
All the blackouts gave me back.

PARABLE WHISTLE

So this guy's walking next to his friend, the snake,
and the snake bites him,
and the guy acts like he can't believe that his friend just bit him,
and his friend says,
"You knew I was a snake."

HURLING CROWBIRDS AT MOCKINGBARS
(HOPE IS NOT A COURSE OF ACTION)

If we were created in God's image,
then when God was a child
He smushed fire ants with His fingertips
and avoided tough questions.
There are ways around being the go-to person,
even for ourselves,

even when the answer is clear,
like the holy water Gentiles would drink
before they realized,

"Forgiveness is the release of all hope for a better past."

I thought those were chime shells in your pocket,
so I chucked a quarter at it
hoping to hear some part of you respond on a high note.
You acted like I was hurling crowbirds at mockingbars,
then abandoned me for not making sense.
Evidently, I don't experience things as rationally as you do.

For example, I know mercy
when I have enough money to change the jukebox
at a gay bar.
You know mercy
whenever someone shoves a stick of morphine
straight up into your heart.
It felt amazing
the days you were happy to see me.

So I smashed a beehive against the ocean
to try and make our splash last longer.
Remember all the honey
had me lookin' like a jellyfish ape,
but you,
you walked off the water
in a porcupine of light,
strands of gold
drizzled out to the tips of your wasps.
This is an apology letter to the both of us
for how long it took me to let things go.

It was not my intention to make such a production
of the emptiness between us,
playing tuba on the tombstone of a soprano
to try and keep some dead singer's perspective alive.
It's just that I coulda swore you sung me a love song back there
and that you meant it,

but I guess some people just chew with their mouth open.

So I ate ear plugs alive with my throat
hoping they'd get lodged
deep enough inside the empty spots
that I wouldn't have to hear you leaving,
so I wouldn't have to listen to my heart keep saying
all my eggs were in a basket of red flags,
all my eyes to a bucket of blindfolds,
in the cupboard with the muzzles and the gauze.
You know I didn't mean to speed so far out and off
trying to drive your nickels to a well
when you were happy to let them wishes drop.

But I still show up for gentleman practice
in the company of lead dancers
hoping
their grace will get stuck in my shoes.
Is that a handsome shadow on my breath, sweet woman,
or is it a cattle call in a school of fish?
Still dance with me,
less like a waltz for panic,
more for the way we'd hoped to swing
the night we took off everything
and we were swingin' for the fences.

Don't hold it against
my love.
You know I wanna breathe deeper than this.
I didn't mean to look so serious.
Didn't mean to act like a filthy floor.
Didn't mean to turn us both into some cutting board.
But there were knives stuck
in the words where I came from.
Too much time in the back of my words.
I pulled knives from my back and my words.
I cut trombones from the moment you slipped away.

And I know it left me lookin' like a knife fight, lady.
Boy, I know it left me feelin' like a shotgun shell.

You know I know I mighta gone and lost my breath.
But I wanna show you how I found my breath to death.
It was buried under all the wind instruments
hidden in your castanets.
Goddamn.
If you ever wanna know how it felt when ya left,
if ya ever wanna come inside,
just knock on the spot
where I finally pressed stop
playing musical chairs with your exit signs.
I'm gonna cause you a miracle
when you see the way I kept God's image alive—

"Forgiveness is for anyone who needs safe passage through my mind."

If I really was created in God's image,
then when God was a boy
He wanted to grow up to be a man,
a good man.
And when God was a man,
a good man,
He started telling the truth in order to get honest responses.
He'd say, "Yeah,
I know …
I really shoulda wore my cross
again,
but I don't wanna scare the Gentiles off."

That is not what I came here to do.
I'm pretty sure, I came here to love you.

WHAT DO YOU PEOPLE DO?

When I was a child,
the first thing I would do upon entering someone's home
is ask them where they kept the toys.
If they said that they did not have any toys
I'd be like, "What the *fuck*?!"

BACKGROUND ON *THE BULLET POINTS*

- My mother's name is Tresa B. Olsen. She is home when I am not.

- Steven Arrowood is my friend. He has a cat named Jim. Jim had cancer of the balls pretty hard but is better now. Steven experiences life clearly and once pointed out that my humor has a tendency to come from a place of anger. Steven has a tendency to come from a place of stupid.

- I have not seen Coach Hendrix from Colonial Village Elementary School in Niagara Falls, New York since the fifth grade. He has likely been shuffled off to the great gig in the sky by now. He had varicose veins in his cheeks. They held up his jowls. Once during kickball, I opted not to peg a runner with the ball, which would have rendered the runner "out." Instead, to make the class laugh, I whipped the ball at Coach Hendrix. I pretended it was an accident. It made him sad and disappointed.

- In "Hurling Corwbirds at Mockingbars," Reverend Kathianne Lewis is responsible for the lines:

   "Forgiveness is the release of all hope for a better past."

   "Forgiveness is for anyone who needs safe passage through my mind."

   She was quoting someone else when she revealed these words, but is nonetheless responsible for passing them forward, and gracefully so. Of any piece I perform, the first of those two lines is most often complimented. I did not write it. Thanks also to my cousin, Lace Williams, who texted me the subtitle *"(Hope is Not a Course of Action),"* which was somehow worked into a conversation where we agreed that the movie *Monsters vs. Aliens* was a bunch of fun.

THAT WAS THEN

DISASTERBATE

"Desperation might be language." – Corbin Bugni

SHOPPING LIST
FOR THE INEFFECTUALLY COPING

Revisionist history back pedals
Homeland insecurity blankets
Selective memory relationship trading cards
Open-hearted surgery blindfolds
Conditioned rubber loves
Unopposable thumb tacks
Diamond ringworm
Spinal tap shoes
Candy canings
Blow torture
Gut wrench
Spilled milk
Nuts
Used group huggies
Double-barreled sawed-off band-aids
Precision-guided phallic symbols
Tender chicken breast strokes
Middle finger applicator with wings

2006 TOUR TEXT

Warble rock jaw.
Chatter thick skull.
Numb Chuck (guy with the tear ducts).
A head still wavering, post gong beat.
Turning my volume in on itself and down.

I grew in these last weeks. More than I would have imagined.
There were such sacred moments. Shared thunder. Shuttering shiverfish.
Watched'm ripple through the room and back. I'm addicted to it.
To giving all the good stuff away but not keeping enough of it safe
at home. More of what I say to people should take a round trip.
Cranking the brightside catapult is an odd job for someone who is
still so uncomfortable with love.
Long stretches of tour create sleep deprivation, even when I've slept.
Here's what I remember:

February 22nd at University of North Florida.
Blue, but I was pushin' black.
Coulda gone up up up
but kept holding back.

February 23rd at University of Michigan.
I was Ian Curtis on love again.

February 24th at Illinois Wesleyan University.
Mind your own isness.

February 25th watching Tim Stafford referee the cage fights near Chicago.
Peel came unwound.
He blew outta the gates swinging pound for pound.
He had the look of war
bolted
to his teeth.

Peel dodged
in out
a hail of the double-edged swords in his doubt.
There's not a lot you can say
to change a mad child's mind.

February 26th at The Green Mill in Chicago.
Ode to the drive and the beat.
Ode to the mountains you move when you speak.

February 27th (day) at Fremd High School in Palatine.
I wrote with firecracker chalk
on a blackboard background

for the wisdom sponge speedball babies.
You?

February 27th (night) at WEEDS in Chicago.
There is no instruction booklet for these balls.

March 3rd at Fire in Kalamazoo.
Fire flighting.
Good eye.

March 7th (day) at Fowlerville Jr. High in Fowlerville.
How can I remember to breathe
when who you are is so exciting?

March 7th (night) at The Heidelberg in Ann Arbor.
Peel Unstable and Inbell Shaker
were eggshell steppers with mallets of yolk.
Now Peel Unstable runs miles of cable
so Inbell Shaker can feathery float.

March 8th (day) at Pioneer High School in Ann Arbor.
There were days of weather strung together
speaking to you that afternoon.

March 8th (night) at The Meta Café in Sturgis.
Gotta slow down
before I wind up
with blood on my teeth
when I can't tell the hunger
apart from release.

RAPID OBSUCCESSION

You said, "Come on in, the water's fine."
So I busted cannonballs off across the ocean and back
and you said, "That's not what I meant."

I know I took things too far sometimes

but I didn't mean to pass you by.

Every day I would try catching up to you.
Every day you would pull me over
and ask where I was going in such a hurry.

By the time I realized I had missed your point
I took to asking if you would meet me, way off the mark.
I'd make you dizzy and hope it felt good.

You're gone now and I get it.
I had to know with my lungs what I did.

Did you see where the wind went
when it got knocked out of me?
Do you know it was by your side?

THE MATH

There are nine red lights on the radio towers at the end of my city.
I can see them from the start of my street.
I don't know how they work
and have only a vague idea of what they do,
but they've been playing that lazy blinking game with me
since I was a child in the backseat
of an adult road trip
to pick up and drop off step-children.
Here's the thing I wondered:

How come my parents couldn't love each other

when all they wanted was to love each other?

It doesn't add up.
I am so much older now
trying to pull the math from my body like a martial art,
making whole numbers out of the fractions they framed me in.
I have been envious of simple formulas

ever since the day I met you,
when my anger got graphed in spheres
and the Pythagoras fell out of my voice,

but I had no idea what he was saying.

I did not retain the kind of information necessary
to stand in your presence and figure remainders.
I retained the way I felt that time I held my breath for 23 years,
not the laws of chemistry
or mechanical engineering.
I do not yet know how to take apart an engine block
or invest in a money system
so I can buy an airplane and fly away
on 75,000 pounds of metal and baggage.

This is my long division.

There were heartbroken cowboys and abandoned women
who I mistook for whole numbers
on the inside of our stereo.
My parents filled the car with them,
tricked me into loving heartache
as if lonely was a thing to strive for.
My FM was nearly beaten to death the day you left.

Subtract this.

When the antenna broke on my parents' car
I listened to mile markers cut past the window
and thought of good hiding places in our house
in case killers came lookin' for a fat kid.
I would have been loads of fun to stab,
porky and fun to stab.
I took out the racks in the oven and hid there
because you didn't think I would.
It takes empathy
and practice

like calculus.

360 degrees.
It got hot in there,
so they kept the car window cracked
to smoke cigarettes and numb the nighttime
while the nighttime shoveled air
into the back seat onto me
like dirty holy moments
blowing down with the smell of
I'm quitting I'm quitting I quit.

It is only necessary to wear a seat belt if you're sitting up.

When a ten-year-old boy lies down
across the bottom half of a leather right angle
traveling 65 mph toward the axis of his parents' choices,
no one bothers him with what will happen
if they swerve across the parallel lines.
Thank goodness I dream too fast
to get killed in a grown-up car crash.

There is a physics to how we fool ourselves.

It is burning steel rods in my envy
when your childhood gets too close to mine.

Here's where I lost your number.

You rode in nice cars with the top down
on your way to speak three language lessons.
They gave you skills you could show off to people,
like how to pole vault and when to let go.
I wanted you to show me X-ray machines
and hand-eye coordination
so I could learn to stop my head before it ran off the road.

Teach me equals.

Tutor me how to not flinch
when I throw my heart in your face.
Let me out of these blinking lights.
Get me out of this whiny car

full of cowboys, and her sadness, and the smoke,
driving sideways, airing out this dirty anger.
Kill a fat kid and his need to be heard.
Let the martyrs
cancel each other out.
Hold me open in a window on the beaches.
Hold me steady to the wealth and on the charm.
No more problems multiplying.
Take my remainders.

I've been hiding

in a dark green Cordoba on the highway
back to before your math could swallow me.
There's not a time I look at a photograph
when some part of my body isn't staring in awe
of how someone like you was able
to figure out the math it took
to take our photograph.
Thanks to the author of the camera,
I have memorized your image when it's still.
I wish you could see what you look like

when you're still here.

ANSWER

"You don't give love in order to get love.
You give love in order to become love." – Apollo Poetry

SEWING QUESTION

Is that your knit pick in my purpose?

ATELOPHOBIA

My closest friends have watched me beat this brain senseless for as long as I can remember, bangin' it against my heart, combin' through the loose skin, makin' a bloody mess, admitting to every recognizable mistake in an effort to come clean, clean, cleaner; frenetic attempts to get it right, stand upright, pseudo-heal a babbling body, swab a swab around inside another wide open wound. Knife fight in my ego. Hyper considerate hate-wad. I know what cards I showed you. I know whose tables they're on. I know how often they've lain there alone. It was my choice to offer you that much information. It's no surprise I want the powers of a boomerang. You shouldn't have given a grinder food for
thought. Stop.

That was then. It was an unnecessary attempt to acknowledge every flaw, confess up every ugly, expose these crooked caves, highlight a habit for fault lines, derail the details, just so I could own it. I owned it, how relentlessly guilty I went, with the hope that if I finally got to be beautiful, no one could hold it against me, that I might deserve arrival, so you won't trade me back for shame.
I didn't want you finding out later
like it matters now. Stop.

I am not here to disrespect your expectations or steamroll anyone's gift. I don't wanna step on your toes. I apologized. For where I came from. For lookin' like that. For spinning out. I spun out on spinning out. I habitually cultivated every single insecurity by thinking it until I spoke it until I lived it until it represented me in towns where I stayed for any longer than a few days. People saw me when I lost the smile inside their 10,000 nitpick questions. I grew so goddamn impatient.
Misfire. Stop.

Desperate greedy beat up brickmouth. I repeated myself again. I re-told where I came from with new words. New distractions. Still believing the story. A river runs rife with guns at the bottom. I tried endearing myself to you from the bottoms up. Guns blazing. Eyes blazing. Words blazing. There are still calluses on my throat from

the day you walked out on my voice. I peeled them back to the root
of envy, stared down the barrel at a tragedy, until all the pinched
skin pulled apart from my hinge. I came unhinged. The weight of
my head collapsed in on itself like a camping cup. I used martyrs for
matches, but love
is not a forest fire. Stop.

I was mad at all the years
I lost on being mad.
Stop.

Unfair is a domino snowball.
Stop.

Stop.

START

I've been lonely for a long time now, hoping anyone who I perceive
as better than me will scoop me up on a night kite rescue mission and
love me so hard that I can finally forget about this feeling left over
from all the years my blood was boiling. Dear Gravel, it doesn't work
like that. If anyone ever loves you that hard, hard as you've been
dreaming, chances are you will not believe them
until you accept yourself.

MERCY IS

… when the universe
doesn't fuck with me
for fuckin' with it.

FOUNDER'S KEEPER

Escape was a rewind button stunt
water falling from the ground back up.
Attach me to any self-portrait
where the back of my head
is mistook for the front.

SELF-PORTRAIT

A Norwegian painter named Odd Nerdrum
paints sick and moist things.
He got lost in the down side of dead
as if dead was a horrible place.
I saw his whole collection of work
in a too-big barbell of a book,
gobbly as his name.
Odd Nerdrum
hurt like a melted pistol whip,
overcooked cream in the middle,
burn victim on a pier,
ice pick bristles and bricks.
He painted the worst hurts of high school
on the walls of my jungle stomach,
warm-blooded balloon in my throat,
pulled apart pencil teeth,
sawed-off chatter slut,
obesity shit on the beach.
It was a dead horse suicide orgy.
Odd Nerdrum painted self-portraits
without the proper postage.
I remember the one of him with a boner.
I found it daring
because he is not a clean man.

It is not brave to be disgusting or unresolved.
I am not proud of a habit to haunt myself
even when it works in the bookends.

I wore my dancing shoes out in the bookends.
I wore a hole in the heel of a canvas,
soiled my sheets of umbilical paper,
self-indulgent self-portrait maker,
an inspired pathetic critic
who would not let it rest. Let it rest,
these honeysuckle sickles,
Odd Nerdrum,
we cannot continue to turn ourselves in
for the mess we left
when we tried coming clean.
I will say it once more and then leave,
from 1974 until 2003
(and some days through 2000 and 10):
I painted ugly self-portraits on purpose
to trail the trigger ditch back to my mother
to show you the fissure they left in her breath
from when they came in to burn out the leech,
from where she planted a man
in her words to protect me.
He was a candy ass maggot wax mustard seed.

Odd Nerdrum,
we are a constellation of starting points
living in the image of a finish line,
but it is not our place to try and keep pace
with all of these things that we wish to feel least.
It is "Build Us an Easier Easel Day"
for dissolving a difficult dream.
It is "Playing a Grand Typewriter Time"
until they call us by our names,
we, runners of the risk of purpose,
my blueberry eye in the smoke,
you hammer the size of a watertrain threaded
through the barrel of a telescope.
Even if they smash our birthmarks off,
they will call us by our names.
I some fancy finger work
and you all the souped-up words your worth.

Odd Nerdrum, we have now been accounted for
and it is written on our empty graves
that *After everything still I stayed.*
And I mean it.
I stayed. I stayed. I stayed.

If there's anything I've come to understand
it's that I left my body to tell you these things
and did not lock the door behind me.
I have told you my story in stencils,
a cut-out image of bread.
It was a rigid appointment with faith
in a barbell of a book.
My name is Buddy Wakefield
and though I have many self-portraits
this is the one of me with a boner.
I find it daring
because I am not a clean man.

FROM *THE DHAMMA BROTHERS*

Ed said, "I don't know if I can do this.
I'm an angry man."

MONKEY ENOUGH
(FOR M.A.R.)

There was a family I dreamed of making
and of loving
driving back roads New York upstate.
Smelt food smoke wood smoke good smoke,
rose up smoke from the chimney,
freshly baked cedar quilt,

haystack tractor porchcan dance,
cobblestone tire swing coverall,
flannel cake.
I was a functional country song in my head some day.
I saw socks rub their feet together on our coffee table
and watched myself watching the playoffs.
You cooked me breakfast.
My children thought I had big hands.
I was not afraid to barbecue for men who understand ballistics.

FLOATING DEVICE

1
Last night I had the same recurring dream where I'm on an airplane
full of babies. They are all wearing very expensive diapers and texting
newspapers back and forth, or playing Sudoku in the full and upright
position. All of them

have become super huffy and passive aggressive pissed off with me
because I can't stop crying like a stabbed cow stuck in a foghorn.
Fuck pretzels.

One of the chubbier huffier babies finally plucks the pacifier out of
his mouth, heaves up a breath from under the silk bib across his vest,
looks directly at me, and says, *"Dude . . . seriously?"*

2
I kick the backs of seats when I don't get the life I need. Do not block
the aisles if I experience absolution. There should be enough room to
dance in it. A room the size of all the wisdom I have so far gathered
up

but have not yet consistently handled well. When I tell you I need to
be alone, what I mean is that I don't want you to see me changing the
batteries on my confidence, or the mercury levels in my floundering.

Bring me back my father. Let us speak of living.

3
My father was a police officer. I wanted to follow in his footsteps so I could legally kick in doors mutherfucker put your hands on my head and hold me

by the greener grass I'm growing, rip out patches from the back and show me

what it is I have to be thankful for.

Remind me.

4
Officer Beasley showed up in my dream with a handful of French burnt peanuts. Those were my favorite when I was a kid. He wouldn't know. He wasn't there.

He held a need to be forgiven on his shoulder. I saw it in his heart. His heart was in my dream. My father's heart was in my dream. It was beating absolutely. He wore it like a badge and I forgave him. Absolutely.

I showed him the bedroom of the man I loved. I showed a need for him to be proud of me. *My father* is proud of me.

The man I loved was not in the room. There was a door on the other side. It was not an emergency exit so I walked through it

5
by myself.

SANBORN, NY

Behind the garage was a stack of cement slabs.

There were skyscraper green construction paper palm leaves taped to the top of four round ice cream buckets, which were stacked up to look like a palm tree.

There were two palm trees.
They were props from a play in Cub Scouts.
I made my mother help me load them
into the back seat of a dark green Cordoba
instead of throwing them away.

When we got home I carried two palm trees
out behind the garage and renamed them
"Ninjas of the Great Green Hair,"
then I beat the shit out of them for sneaking up on me.

We had a flag pole and a gravel driveway.
My mother did yard work and I did room to wander.
I used a turquoise aluminum bat with a black rubber handle.
I batted gravel to the cornfield.
I batted a softball through two garage window panes
for the same reason I'll stick a spoon through crème brûlée.

There was a tree in the corner of the cornfield
where I told myself secrets I did not keep.
I have not taken time to hold any tighter.
Such a monster was made of those days
I nearly forgot about the grapevine and clothesline,
the brand new yellow aluminum siding.

Thank you for the room with five windows
and for the foam mattresses
so I could wrestle the whole neighborhood,
and for the dining room chairs
so I could wrestle the whole neighborhood
from the top turnbuckle.

Mom, were you pinned under cookie dough and blood back there?

Did you know that when the snow came
I used a stack of cement slabs
to climb to the roof of the garage?
Did you know I would have invited you up
and pointed out a tree with my bat
where you could go to get ready

for the violence we caused ourselves?

THE SIZE AND SHAPE
OF ALL THINGS ROLLING

By the time my fingernails had split
and cut their way back in toward the knuckle grit
I had already chewed these teeth
clear down to the dirty nubs
from chattering about how hard I hit bottom again,
how far I had to climb up out of it,
shovel myself off and start over.
Been doin' that long as I can remember,
as if it were my calling,
as if my name were Helter Skelly,
rising from falls I keep taking in vain
just for a reason to stand here
lookin' like another loose jawbone
hinged on a Tilt-A-Whirl.

The question was,
"If God can do anything,
can he can make a rock so big
that even He can't lift it?"

The answer is, "Yes,
all He has to do
is commit to defeating himself."

BRAWL

Today
I got into a bar fight in my head

that I could not possibly win.
But I did.
I did win.

IN PURSUIT OF ARRIVING

"Tell me that my brothers will forgive me for kicking to the surface of the sea." – Tara Hardy

JEAN HEATH

In the end
Jean Heath's home was filled with people who claimed to know her
better than they actually did.
They swapped tissues and embellished stories
to appear closer to Jean Heath than they actually were,
in the same way
wearing expensive clothes on Sunday
apparently brings wealthy Baptists
closer to God than they actually are.

It was mostly unfamiliar faces who seemed
to be looking for due credit
on the role they may or may not have played
in the life of Jean Heath,
networking their sorrow and searching
like they always do in every death
for the gate to restoration,
as if this life
really wants us to stay here.

They took turns crying on Jean Heath's face
as a sign she would be missed.

There was so much crying that I, the caregiver,
could hear Jean Heath's bed sheets
slap together when she moved.
And there was food.
Holy hams and jam, y'all, there was so much food.
At least an acre of it.
Across the kitchen countertops and over the tables,
falling out of the refrigerator and along the arms of chairs.
There were plastic cups with names written on them.
Sometimes twice. Sometimes two cups.
Kids lose shit.

There was ambrosia with snot on it,
cornbread with tears in it,
black-eyed peas with the trembling ladle,
strawberry rhubarbed wire pie,
melty vanilla ice creamed pulp
and there were perfect middle squares still left in the brownie pan.
I know who ate the end pieces.
The little ones were warned
death is a very serious matter,
so they had better not act up or else they would be forced
to pick their own switch and get whipped with it.

We were tricked
into fearing the ways we will leave this planet.

Emily Beezhold was 26 years old that day when she came to play piano
for her best friend Jean Heath, age 87,
who lay flat and velvet on her death bed
lookin' like the front pew of a gospel church without the guilt.
When the other guests asked Emily how she knew Jean Heath,
Emily thought of Jean's lonely days on the porch
when no one came to visit,
when the money ran out,
when the yearning for love haunted her,
taught her how heavy the hollows are,
how crippled a memory can make ya,
how sometimes she'd cry so hard her throat locked out all the noise.
"I trust you people

about as far as I can throw you,"
Emily said,
"and I can't throw you."

The candles inside her piano keys are why
Emily's fingertips burn when she plays.
It's why she plays like that.
It doesn't scare Jean Heath when she plays like that.
She bangs both feet down on the sustain pedal bouncing
and she sings like that,
teeth all gripped out like a hallway howling.
Holler holler, she sang,
I'm goin' home.
Might be
a little bit bit but
I'm gonna show'm.
Might be dirty
might be skinny like water
but there's a hole in god
and I'm not gonna fall down in there.

And that day when she played,
sometimes with her knuckles,
mostly with her memory,
she remembered a true story she read once
in a book about self-acceptance
where a daughter sits next to her mother who's in a coma
until one morning before dawn
when the mother wakes up,
looks very clearly and very intently at her daughter,
and says, "Ya know,
my whole life, I thought there was something wrong with me."
Then the mother shook her head as if to say,
What a waste
before drifting back into her coma and dying
several hours later.

You knew she would.
These stories we give each other are just different reasons
for begging you to stay

but nobody's gonna stay here.
Emily knows Jean Heath won't stay.
She's cool with that.
They both just wish they would've known a little sooner about this life
that every loss doesn't have to cost so much,
doesn't have to hit so heavy,
doesn't have to get so dirty.

Dirty dirty like Christ
on his little brown mule.
I was baptized in tap water
and I never really went to school.
I got a hunger for ya
I got a hunger for you
but I never
but I never
but I never really came through.

Jean Heath was tender and bossy when she finally
called Emily Beezhold to her bedside.
While she was happy
that her house smelled like a baked good
and she was thankful
for the best of the gestures from the guests in the bedrooms
and she was wondering about some of the recipes,
Jean Heath was very clear and very intent
in the moment she finally pulled Emily Beezhold's ear
down to her mouth
and said inside of it,

"Get these people out of my house.
I've never died before.
And I'm gonna enjoy it."

SOURCES FOR *THAT WAS THEN*

- I saw a 16-year-old boy named Corbin Bugni perform a poem while at a Youth Speaks Seattle event. In that poem he paused like a man and invited the crowd to break into his prayer. *Break into my prayer.* Corbin and his peers at Youth Speaks are proof that psychological evolution is happening. Years later I heard him acknowledge that desperation might be language. For a moment, I was solved.

- "Shopping List for the Ineffectually Coping" was highly inspired by David la Terre, who I knew as Tin Tin, who was a staple in the Seattle poetry scene when I began in 1998. He claimed he got beat up a lot. I understood why. As did he.

- I was house-sitting for a friend. There was an art gallery on Main Street in Venice Beach called Obsolete. I would go inside with wheels on the heels of my shoes. There I saw a too-big barbell of a book which contained the works of a Norwegian painter named Odd Nerdrum. I sent it to Tiffany Hill because she was the one who had shown me his ferocious talent. I wanted her to see all of him. Tiffany Hill has seen all of me. If it were not for her when we were young and often alone, I may not have stayed.

- It is no secret that my life is righted by Vipassana. *The Dhamma Brothers* is a movie about prisoners taking the 10-day Vipassana course. When prisoner Ed said, "I don't know if I can do this, I'm an angry man… " I began to weep.

- Kenneth Zane Beasley, Jr. was my father.

- Tara Hardy and I began our performance poet careers at the same time in the same place at The OK Hotel in Seattle. I become significantly happy inside for her successes. She and Ryler Dustin are the most prolific, quality spoken word writers I can think of. Tara Hardy once reminded me what I carry on behalf of my kind. Twice.

- "Jean Heath" was entirely based on the last lines of said poem. While the names and quotes used are real, the details of the situation are imagined. Two verses from the song "Skinny Like

Water" are courtesy of Timmy Straw. The story of the woman
in the coma is paraphrased from Tara Brach's book *Radical
Acceptance*.

ALL THE WATER BACK

HORSEHEAD

When I rode off into the sunset,
there was no blackout
or camera behind me.
I did not recede into the distance.
I was still very much present
with what I had left behind.
My horse was thirsty
from how far I ran him,
and your God as my witness,
I ran him,
until I rode into town here and realized
I am not the end of a movie.

I am done playing sunsets for lonely.
My best days are the days I see clearly.
So I had hoped
to come clean here perfectly
for you and the whole saloon,
but there is no polish on the table tonight.
Expect rough spots then
when I show you my cards.
These hands we were dealt
may splinter.
The spades could get under your skin.
I was livin' with'm under my skin.
They were digging up into my film strip.
I was ridin' with'm stuck in my heart.

It is work to ride head up and holy here.
It is painters with slack in their brush,
painters all jacked up
on stampede dust
just trying to get it right.
I've been trying to get it right.
I've been learning here how to grow larger
than the monsters alive in my dreams;

swinging a crow bar
out of my whistle,
grand pianos out of my rust,
I shot typewriter keys out of cannons I keep
aimed at the bandits alive in my trust.

There were bandits alive in my trust
come to burn down the verbs
left alone in my blood
barkin' like dogs in a combine,
my horsehead sweat
like a war on a land mine,
jawbone chomp at the bit
like a bear trap telegraph;
I know I look
like a bleeding dot
by now from where you stand
where there is mad dash
and such wild west
and it is raining down locomotives on a horse
who might not have a name
but who carries a trough in his chest,
empty as it may be today
from feeding bandits disguised as the Pony Express.
Comin' up spades and splinters,
my workhorse spittin' out hammers and ink—

there is a colony of bad fathers
who built this place
still alive in the way I was led to think,
like a snake
who can shed its own crucifixion,
or a midnight rider
who leaves his beast
under whip of the daylight sky;
that's why I looked like gallop cursive
when you held me under
the horizon line
to magnify

every single silver screen I stole
riding high on my filthy electric whale
like a bullet through a junkyard ghost.
Ya know,
I don't care to be good, Sheriff.

I care to be whole.

So read what it says in my buckles, boy:
Take your sunset out of my rise.
I will not send you sailing if you came here to drive,
and I know you came here to drive.
That's why it reads *Don't Give Up* on your saddle,
like I wrote *Won't Give Up* on my life,
like I've been typing my name
on a horse I drove
through the desert as sure as a river he ran,
and I swear on my shadow he wouldn't turn back
no matter how much slack I typed into his neck.
Not everyone wants to go home

to get the sunset painted back into their bones,

to have the law with all that slack in its love

pretending to save me.

You don't need to save me.

I already did that myself

when your God as my witness

never turned up.

There was a typewriter

buried alive in that horse,

the one I rode to get out of the flood.

IT HAPPENED

The glass was cleaned for them.

A scene spread out like privacy
clear corner of a schoolyard children
move upward safe in bird slopes
in warm spots
on a break in the clouds
a picture of a picture smiling
smart families holding on
thick sweaters and schoolbooks
backpacks filled with porch swings
a future courtyard's wide
fountain in a marble ballroom
bundled in the music hall
comfortable starfish story
circling ripples outward
reassurance in the air
they all felt sharp and crisp
bread baskets
spilling talent spiders out of their eyes
crawling into me
rich like the mothers
who had enough arms to raise them.

CIRCUMLOCUTION

—noun
"A roundabout or indirect way of speaking; the use of more words
than necessary to express an idea." – Dictionary.com

IRIS

If bright pink and bright orange
developed into one color
with yellow
heightened, diminished, or opened in the black,
that's what I see when I close my eyes.
Iris, get in here.
Tell me how much the light got through.
Relax your language.
Just say what you see.
I saw a hand held up,
rooted at the wrist like a tree
built from staircases.
I climbed to the tip of the ring finger
and made myself a promise
to cross the finish line
as is
no matter what
this too.
When I say my ABC's
there is a series of descending movements
deeply sideways from A to Z.
The way from L to P writes just like a waterslide, Iris,
you caught me halfway home.
I already know what color my house is
on the inside.

WHO LEFT THIS HERE?

When there's a mountain standing in my way,
it's not personal.

WATER GUN

You approached me like a molehill
in the hour of my mountain.
There was a shovel tucked
into the small of your crooked back
where the water guns used to go
and I didn't see you reach for it, Squirt.

When I welcomed you in,
trust came first.
There was no need for a cavity search.
You took advantage of this and hid
an entire sandcastle deconstruction kit
right behind that big bright eye,
tried tunneling through me like an ulcer
in my child side.

I don't go lookin' for snake bites on breathing tubes,
but there you were,
teeth sunk in,
caught red no-handed and rattled.
Ya got rattled when I caught ya,
became irrational when I caught ya,
like a balloon we filled up and let loose.

It was easy for you to take the wind out of my sails.
All you had to do was suck.
You're so clever
the way you slit the big out of people
then pat them on the fault lines.
Remember when I would scratch your back
then you would hold up my weakness and stab it
with the backscratcher?

Felt like a child again
the way we both let me hate myself
as hard as I possibly could.
I still look just like you in the mirror some days,

still talk like you when the time's right,
with that flashy dance floor tongue
and your slicked back mirror ball face
reflecting all the ways you would destroy yourself
if there was no one else around.

You finally wore out the welcome mat,
wiped off your feet on my door like that,
arms spread out like an abacus
saying I could count on you.
I ended up with zero
watching those loose lips slide sunk ships
back and forth across your expiration date.

You built a corner around me
because I couldn't be backed into one,
stared down the barrel of a cheap shot
and pointed it straight at my smile.
Gunning down easy targets is for beginners, Billy Kid.
There is no high noon in my heart today.
You will not shoot holes in the dam.
People drink here.

Stand there and call it my life if ya wanna.
Trigger every inch of my spine.
This spine will not quit my blood when it's boiling.
My blood was not built to rest.
You can leave that up to my breath.
This breath is the fairest way.
It is the only instrument left on stage
I came to this world fully knowing
how to string and tune up,
strum and reload,
whistle and fiddle, harpoon it and play.

If living
really is the greatest revenge,
then I want you to know my breath.

And if we really do get what we give,

then I give up,
so I can get up.

A HISTORY OF *ALL THE WATER BACK*

- I wrote "Horsehead" committed like a nine-to-five job at the O.C.D. for three months on Amber Tamblyn's dining room table. There was a giant ceramic horse head pointed straight up at the sky (sculpted by Amy Evans, wife of Michael McClure) and an ancient typewriter. They were sitting next to each other. They were set up on the Los Angeles end of the table. I sat at the Pacific Ocean end of the table, facing them. There were three songs playing on repeat. Sometimes the songs repeated together, sometimes I programmed them to repeat alone. They were:

  "I'm No Heroine" by Ani DiFranco
  "Midnight Rider" by Willie Nelson
  "Polly Come Home" by Robert Plant and Alison Krauss

  Utah Philips is alive in this work.

- "Water Gun" is dedicated to a few spitting images of me whose names need not be mentioned. I've likely been guilty of anything I can accuse them.

CEASE CONVINCING REST ASSURED

WE'RE ALL IN THIS TOGETHER

"Ya know man, I find that the mere act of engaging in conversation is enough to put me in fight or flight mode." – Ani DiFranco

"The best thing I learned in my science course in college: *energy cannot be created or destroyed.* It was an a-ha moment when I remembered there was nothing to fear. Everything is in the universe forever. Together." – Joe Kowalke

"When you're done healing this and that, come thrive with me." – Rev. Kathianne Lewis

MARCH 14, 2006
FINALLY HOME IN SEATTLE

On my bedroom wall there is artwork of a baboon on a stool looking sincere and tired,
and printed underneath him is the word "survivors."

Today I did an image search on the word "livers"
then I printed the clearest picture of a liver
and hung it next to the baboon.

OCTOBER 15, 2009
GREATEST DAY EVER DAY

Today when I got off the plane
from Baltimore into Dallas-Fort Worth Airport,
CNN was plastered at every gate with breaking news.
There was a 6-year-old boy zoomin' 8,000 feet through the sky and the clouds
in a helium balloon his dad had been working on,

and while the crap yackers shook their buzzard heads
and the tragedy addicts spoke their doomed thoughts
and some people laughed with wonderment,
I felt my entire body light up like an extra gumball that came down for free.
Oh my goodness.
Myyy gooodness dear God of all that is *awesome*, would ya look at that…
An ocean of tree houses surged up and filled me over into next person
and I imagined that boy's giant eyes widening up his life
riding all that vast miraculous
and I don't care if he really was just hiding in a box in the attic.

WHEN A GUN BEGINS TO BE GUN

Once, I stayed after church to join a prayer circle because I was
concerned about the way I unlove people.

The circle was all women with soft voices holding hands,
eyes closed.

Each woman would pray thanks then pass to the next person with a
slight squeeze to her left.

When she squeezed my right hand I began to speak. My deep voice
accidentally crushed out and tackled the soft space. I felt the room
stop.

Only one thought spread through me in the pause before I continued
praying out loud with them:

Do not let every man who ever came before you speak for you now.

JANUARY 10, 2009
SONGS IN THE KEY OF CROWBAR

Last night I had a dream there was an ex-con sitting at a cafeteria table facing forward in a large room full of maybe one hundred other folks who were also facing forward on their cafeteria table bench seats.
He was dressed in plain clothes, but I knew, because my dream told me, that he had just gotten out of prison. He was sitting toward the back of the room.
He stood up without any prompting and began to talk some wisdom loudly.
The other folks were either embarrassed for him
or not paying attention at all
or looking at him with fear.
The only thing I can remember from his outburst was at the end
when he dug his chin into his chest, curled his body inward a little bit
then a little bit more, then began saying
something louder and louder, and louder and louder
until he finally fully unfolded, opening his whole body up
little by little by little, more and more
as he heaved it, in exaltation, in joy,
in pure joy, like he was birthing it finally,
not just saying it, but knowing it
and sharing it....
What I have...

What I have.

What I have.
What I Have.
What I Have!

What I Have!!

What I Have!!!

WHAT I HAVE!!

WHAT I HAVE!!!

WHAT I HAVE!!!
WHAT I HAVE!!!
WHAT I HAVE!!!
WHAT I HAVE!!!!
WHAT – I – HAVE!!!!

WHAT – I HAVE!!!!
WHAT – I HAVE!!!!
WHAT I – HAVE!!!!!!!
WHAT I HAVE!!!!!!!
WHAT I HAAVE!!!!!!!

WHHAAAT IIII HAAAVE!!!!!

WHHAAAT IIIII HHAAAVVEE!!!!!!

WWHHHAAATT I HHAAAAAAVVEE!!!!!!!!!!!

What I,

Have

FREE ADMISSION

At the Woodland Park Zoo, Lindsey Buchan and I walked into a giant birdcage accessible also to the humans. Inside, we saw a bird called *Violaceous Turaco*. The first note listed on the informative plaque in its cage read:

Awkward while airborne.

PROLOGUE

Step into this experience
with the goose bumps
in your heartbeat
and your good graces
and your fashionable unoriginality
and your appreciation for *Where the Wild Things Are*
(if you did not have an emotional reaction to that movie,
I wish you luck finding your soul).

Here's to all of us
letting go of the distractions,
warding off the worries,
forgetting your shitty boss
and the work load
or any bad advice ya mighta got today.

If you've been in a relationship you don't know how to get out of...
    not tonight.
Forget about the way you may have settled for looks and made up the rest.
Tonight is your night.
Give it a rest.
Just rest.
Like, if you've got a yeast infection ...
tonight you do not.

Leave all those things out of your mind,
out of your reason,
out of this room,
off of this street,
and away from this city,
in a place you will never visit.
Let's learn something new together, shall we?

Let's think about what can go right tonight.
Receive what you believe.
There is no need to internalize the chaos.
It will still exist without you.
Take your hands off the controls.
Stop holding on with your neck so tight.
We're all in this together.

WE WERE EMERGENCIES

We can stick anything into the fog
and make it look like a ghost.
But tonight,
let us not become tragedies.
We are not funeral homes
with propane tanks in our windows,
lookin' like cemeteries.
Cemeteries are just the Earth's way of not letting go.
Let go.

Tonight,
let's turn our silly wrists so far backwards
the razor blades in our pencil tips
can't get a good angle on all that beauty inside.
Step into this
with your airplane parts.
Move forward,
and repeat after me with your heart:

"I no longer need you to fuck me as hard as I hated myself."

Make love to me
like you know I am better
than the worst thing I ever did.
Go slow.
I'm new to this.
But I have seen nearly every city from a rooftop
without jumping.
I have realized

that the moon
did not have to be full for us to love it,
that we are not tragedies
stranded here beneath it,
that if my heart
really broke
every time I fell from love,
I'd be able to offer you confetti by now.

But hearts don't break,
y'all,
they bruise and get better.
We were never tragedies.
We were emergencies.
You call 9-1-1.
Tell them I'm having a fantastic time.

LITTLE STINKER OR JOHNNY GOT HIS BUN

As I rounded 2nd Ave NW onto 72nd Street
he had already planted the seed
and his hand.

He was casual about it.
He did it without thinking.
He did it without knowing I was turning the corner

or that I would see him
in one long crooked swoop
reach a hand down into the back of his pants,
stick it between his butt
(tip of forefinger spotting about),
then yank that hand upward
until the last few inches of space just before his face
where he delicately brought the situation to his nose.

It is safe to say he was briefly lost on the inhale.
It was quite a long sniff indeed.
I had to double check
that he wasn't holding a flower.

His eyes blew open at the sound of my car
but by then it was too late
for either of us
to back pedal out of this permanent scar.

We locked eyes through my windshield
both slightly mortified.
I less so.
More concerned than mortified, really.

I have been known to be too honest.
It comes honest.
I mean to make things better
when I lay my cards on the table.
It's not to insult anyone
or make them uncomfortable.
This quality often goes unappreciated
as was the case on this day
when I threw my car in park
and jumped out of it
perhaps a bit too aggressive,
jogged over to the neighborhood boy
and crouched down,
put my hand on his shoulder
(politely asking him to not touch me with his left hand)
and said, "Hey, listen…

it's *okay*.
We all do the hand-to-butt, butt-to-nose thing.
Nothing wrong just happened.

"One time I shoved a drum stick up my butt
just to see how far it would go, ya know,
so seriously, don't worry about it.
It's not like I'm gonna tell the other kids
or your mom or dad or somethin'.
It's just a funny little reminder that we should look around first.
But really, who cares?

"Check it out, this other time when I was six,
I peed in a Tupperware bowl and...
Don't worry, it's not what you think. I didn't drink it.
But it's cool with me if that's your thing.
Anyhow, there was this repair guy fixing our washing machine
which was in the bathroom
and for some reason
I was too embarrassed to ask to go to the bathroom,
so I peed in a bowl in my room upstairs
then dumped it out the window onto the pantry roof.
When I shoved the window back down to shut it
all eight of my pudgy little fingers got jammed in the sill.
I screamed like a fucking bat orgy until my mom
came running upstairs to lift the window for me
and uncrush my fingers.

"She had a lot of questions
like about why I had the window open in winter
and why were my pants down
and where was the other drumstick.
I finally had to tell her,
'Mom, I dumped a bowl of pee onto the pantry roof,'
which totally would not have been a big deal
if she hadn't just caught me earlier that week
trying on my stepdad's underwear.

"Dude, I'm an embarrassing moments magnet.
People are compelled to do awfully strange things,

natural or not. Some super incredibly awkward strange things, really…

When I was in 7th grade
I prayed for wisdom while I was taking a shit.
Seriously, I was on the toilet
praying
to Jesus
for wisdom
while pumpin' out the jams.
That's twisted. I mean,
when you get to the 7th grade,
if you even pray at all,
it's gonna be for like a girlfriend
or a hand job, right?

"I may be *the* oddest feller I know,
so seriously, boss,
don't get tripped up on the fact that
I just saw you smell your ass with your hand,
ya know what I mean? I mean
now ya know, yeah?
It's pungent as all get out, right?
Surprising pungent too.
You'll probably even check again sometime
just to be sure it really smells that strong.
But it's cool, kid. You're secret's safe with me.
In the big picture of things,
smellin' your own ass is no big secret.
It's all good in the hood, man."
Then I pointed at him real awkward
in an attempt to show him I was down,
"You know…in moderation."
Then I laughed.
He didn't.
"Jus' kiddin'."
I slapped him on the shoulder.
"You cool? I'm cool.
I feel good about this."

I leaned back.

The neighborhood boy,
whose face I never saw again,
looked up at me,
his eyes the size of a bad speech,
sinking back into that dirty little head of his
which ever so slowly shook itself
side to side
while his thoughts
tried to pull his body back out of paralysis.
He let out one long chunky weep of a breath.
A sliver of spittle
slapped down across his quivering chin.

He backed up,
breaking free from my gentle hold,
turning in every way,
then ran off unevenly
along the sewer line between two houses,
choppy, clompy, klutzy steps
that kept causing a hiccup of terrified reverse gulps
to burst up between the weezy peeps
of a very strange boy indeed.

A CONVERSATION I WITNESSED AT BUMBERSHOOT HEADQUARTERS

WOMAN IN CHARGE OF RADIOS: Hey, there he is!

GUY WITH BLACK EYE: Hi.

WOMAN IN CHARGE OF RADIOS: Oh, and you got your braces off!

GUY WITH BLACK EYE: Yeah, three years ago, but you say that every year.

WOMAN IN CHARGE OF RADIOS: Well, just look at those pearly whites!

A POINT OF COMPLETE

I like you,
but sometimes
it can take me a while to admit it to myself.

STRIPPED DOWN PASSED NAKED TO THE WATER BELOW

CHRISTA BELL: Does your family consider you the black sheep?

ELLEN GEARY: Ya know, if they do, at this point, it's like, I am love, and if that's weird for you. . . .

AUGUST 18, 2010
PREPARATION 8

Dear Proposition 8, Mormons, and Orange County,

I officiated the wedding of a straight couple on Sunday and I was thinkin' . . . I've been known to be pretty gay. Shouldn't this mean their marriage not be recognized? Isn't the sanctity of a straight couple at risk if they're married by a gay dude? Shouldn't straight marriages performed by gay dudes be revoked as a safeguard against burning forever? Please help me help you help God help us, or before ya know it they'll be letting murderers and animals officiate . . . maybe even priests. Something more must be done to stop the spread of joy, and butt sex.

Looking to You for Christlike Moral Guidance Because You and Your Divorce Rates Representing Sanctity Totally Make Sense,

Reverend B. Wakefield

P.S. I feel like y'all should go after the Universal Life Church next, to put an end to the possibility of openly human/gay people presiding over straight weddings. Once that's accomplished, we can begin voiding the millions of marriages performed by such ambiguous clergy. It's a purification process, and should serve to bring the human race closer together. It may seem like de-evolution or Hitleresque at first, but I for one understand that you have books to live by, like— say—the Bible, which clearly states all sins are measured equally. For instance, if I call you a retarded ape, that's a sin, unless you truly are a retarded ape, which...
At any rate, please stop.
Abort this hateful mission (and I don't mean the kids you may be raising).

INROADS TO
CEASE CONVINCING REST ASSURED

- While opening for Ani DiFranco in Omaha, Nebraska, I lost
  myself to a panic on stage in front of hundreds of folks. No one
  was heckling or being malicious. People were just getting drunk
  and loud in the back. I felt like a dancing monkey. I stopped
  what I was doing and asked "What the fuck?" out loud, of
  everything, then I did my last piece and walked to the bus. In
  the moment when I expected to see her most disappointed, Ani
  ran up and hugged me well, laughing a little victoriously, and
  thanked me for being a real live human.

  Outside of The Granada in Dallas, there was a parked car with
  ANI DIFRANCO plastered on a sticker across the bumper.
  Ani was sitting next to me on the bus as I stared at it. I looked
  over at her and joked, "You're a bumper sticker." She looked at
  the bumper sticker, then back at me and slowly said, "Yeah." I
  immediately felt wonky for saying it out loud, especially because
  she knows I make fun of bumper stickers in an old piece I wrote.
  Later, backstage, I said, "Ani, I don't ever need to justify or
  qualify myself or the awkward things that may come out of my
  mouth to you, do I?" She smiled and said, "Nah, I got you. You
  work out whatever it is you're workin' out." I had forgotten
  that if you help revolutionize women in music, you might get a
  bumper sticker or two.

  When I told Ani I was in love (the real kind; not the desperate
  burning thing I used to called love) she was elated that I "found
  the transcendental welcome mat." She is raw grace on and off the
  stage. She is also the reason I can leave the road and feel complete
  about my career as a performance poet. I don't know if you ever
  dreamt of rolling down the highway on a tour bus at 3 am, but I
  did. And I got to. Thank you, Ani.

- Reverend Kathianne Lewis is thanked multiple times in this book for her constant reminders of what matters most to my journey. Her sermons keep me healthy. If ever in Seattle, Washington, on a Sunday or Wednesday, you'll be well received at the Center for Spiritual Living on Sandpoint Way.

- Bob Houston of Bellingham, Washington, turned me on to the understanding that today is "Greatest Day Ever Day." Bob is one of the quick-wittiest people I have the honor of knowing. His contributions and maintenance of the Northwest poetry scene are limitless and indispensable. I'm lucky to have him as a friend. He once said something like, "Just because everyone else loves something, doesn't make my love of it any less of a miracle. I love it." I'll not soon forget that moment, or what was on the table when you said it, Bob.

- The photo from the end of the "Songs in the Key of Crowbar" journal entry was taken the moment Obama was elected. The title for that entry is by Anis Mojgani. Anis Mojgani is the gentleweight champion of the world. Mike McGee told me so.

- Lindsay Buchan and I met at a crossroads. She called me Sunny Buns and I collected things for her to do with one arm. We bought season passes to the zoo and jogged around Green Lake until she met the love of her life. When we have dinner with her fiancé and our mutual friends, we tend to catch each other's eyes a lot and silently laugh about the party we know is going on somewhere right now, and that we could totally crash it if we wanted.

- Ted Whalen is responsible for calling 9-1-1 to say he was having a fantastic time.

- I was volunteering at a Vipassana course when I heard Christa Bell and Ellen Geary have the documented conversation. Light switches work.

- Oh, and Joe Kowalke. Joe Kowalke and me, we're 100%.

JANUARY 18, 2008
AN ONGOING ACCOUNT OF WAKING UP

There are a lot of movies I wouldn't be ashamed to call my favorite:
Gummo
Lonesome Dove
Magnolia
Secretary
Georgia
Waking Life
Transamerica
Brazil
Men Don't Leave
Delicatessen
Me and You and Everyone We Know
Sling Blade
I kinda wanna compulsively sit here and make a list of dozens of movies,
but the point is that when a movie does its job 100%,
well, then it's 100%.
It doesn't get fuller than 100%.
100% is 100%, right? It's complete.
110% is an alternate reality
born out of an insatiable place like passion.
But when I get too lazy to explain this and I declare only one favorite movie,
I say *The Shawshank Redemption*.
Doesn't mean there aren't a hundred more movies with 100% impact.
The Shawshank Redemption just happened to do it for me first.

The same idea also applies to my "best" friend(s).

It also applies to days:
The day after my first show with Ani DiFranco, wandering Earthdance Festival.
The first eight days in Rotterdam.
The day in college I spent suspending judgment.
The night I got stoned to Bone Machine by Tom Waits.
The day alone at Enchanted Rock in Fredericksburg, TX.
The day I understood what a moment does, in Lake Forest, IL.
Day 11 of my first Vipassana experience.

The day with Kealoha in Hawaii.
Edinburgh with Andrea and Katie and Leigh.
Sledding with Dogger, Shona, and Rose into board games and hot cocoa and nighttime.
Camping with Remond and Squid and Carrie and Seth and Shona and Surgue.
I wanna list dozens more favorites again
but I know my firstborn favorite day declared was July 27, 1997.
Nicole Appel, Daniel Plunkett, me, and Joe Kowalke.

We had left Stanford University that morning
armed with backpacks full of wigs and capes and water guns,
candy and French fries, and affirmations that we'd written down on napkins
like **"THIS IS IT!"**
and **"If the sun or moon should doubt, they would immediately
go out." – William Blake**

We boarded the Caltrain headed for San Francisco.
We slipped into the necessary gear for a proper
random act of kindness stick-up,
then when enough unsuspecting passengers
were snug en route,

I stood up,
water gun pointed in the air
and yelled,
"Nobody move! This is a random act of kindness stick-up!
Let us be nice to you and no one will get squirt!"
My three superfriends launched out of their seats yellin' things like,
"Whatever you dream you can also accomplish!"
and
"What would you do if you knew you couldn't fail?!"
and
"TAKE THE CANDY!"
and
"Eat these French fries, lady! We've got ketchup!"

People were stumped.
Purses were clutched.
It happened so fast
few had time to make sense of us.
We were exhilarated.
Emptied of our kindness supplies,
we raced back to our four seats and faced each other,
pretty weirded out and proud of ourselves,
breathing heavy,
not really knowing what to do next,
acting as if.

I remember one woman clapping from her seat
and saying loud enough for us to hear,
"Great job, you guys!"

We passed through the city of San Francisco that day
on just our laughter and seized moments
from the Wharf to Haight-Ashbury,
where we took to chasing through the woods
gravitating toward what sounded like some sort of
Universe Yes dance
like Armageddon went and got stoned,
pulled us out into the clear and laughed, like windows do.
There was a path for each of us
as we ran and we ran ran ran

over every mud-packed uproot
then suddenly out into a massive green clearing where a man sat
surrounded by dirty and colorful people
singing about the purpose.

And here I am again in the clearing.

2007 ended for me tonight at Brandeis University
where there was such poetry
and a crowd who showed up in thunder.
My original spoken word inspirado spoke. Saul Williams
is still Saul Williams (like amazing still means amazing
even if people use the word too much)
and I'm still a wide-eyed wandering baby lookin' up most days,
but today, I have finally arrived at 2008,
eighteen days later and alive and well,
honored by full circle,
fresh off an electric show,
still realizing a dream.
My third course into silence through Vipassana (*www.dhamma.org*)
lasted from December 27th thru January 6th,
so on January 1st there was no communally celebrated New Year
or an agreement to move forward with fireworks.
Tonight there was.

The thought of recapping 2007 shuttles my brain into traction.
2007 straight up spanked me
like my mom did when I said "Fuck you"
to my seventh grade science teacher, Mr. Brown.
I felt way too old for the whoopin', but we (my mom, me, and 2007)
had our reasons for doing some of the things we did.
I still hit this year up for lunch money and loved it for the learning,
respected the vessel, had no doubt it was loving me back.
2007 dangled me out over the highway
into nonstop solo touring February through April,
into the tour with Derrick Brown,
into being seven sardines on the "Human the Death Dance Tour"
for two months,
into National Finals into more solo shows,
straight into another full van of six on

"Solomon Sparrow's Electric Whale Revival,"
straight onto the bus with Ani DiFranco,
then directly over to Europe with the "I Am A Lagan Tour" through
December, directly into Vipassana.

I like to be alone a lot.
2007 absolutely did not have that in the cards
until the end.
In the end it was my favorite tour.
In every sense of that statement.
I've been blessed with (and have created) a lot of experiences
where I was able to work in team situations for long periods of time
with vulnerabilities exposed under intense pressures,
but 2007, you sweet ferocious, you taught me best.
Back in June I started to find out how hard a blessing can punch a person.
During the "Human the Death Dance Tour," I began to notice
what felt like a swollen nerve inside the crook of my elbow
running through my bicep into my shoulder and under the back blade.
About eight months later (last week),
I realized I would not be able to do the physical training I'd been planning
if I didn't get it taken care of, so I went to a neurological masseuse.
She pressed some pressure points, pulled some triggers,
released the torrent of toxicity I'd been storing
right
there
and sent me on my way.

The next day I felt like I had the flu.
The day after that I woke up with a black eye (no kidding);
there was an inch-long patch of purple blood blister right there under my eye.
That same day on the flight to Salt Lake City I got a bloody nose
and it felt like someone was literally welding inside my arm.
As I sat there with a black eye and bloody nose dripping, arm on fire
while a woman—who told me I reminded her of her son—fed me Kleenex,
I grinned awful big, feeling every bit 2007,
huge enough for me to look at in detail
worthy enough to be let go.

If a movie were being filmed inside my left arm that day
it would've been motion shots of a cactus

(how a cactus sometimes looks like it's flipping off the sun
trying to stab it a thousand times)
being run over by a river of tour buses
rapidly leaving my body. Left behind:
just my vital organs
and the Lagans
and my grown-up thoughts
like sobriety
and the realization that I ended 2007
100%, like Joe Kowalke and me.

Maybe the movie inside my body
had finally zeroed in on the strutting lion,
big cocky king of the jungle,
makin' his way across some coastline
he'd never been before.
And as the camera zoomed out we saw that lion completely unaware
that he was walking into the wide open mouth of a whale
and the whale was closing his mouth, smiling,
smiling even if the ocean dries up
and even if the sun that will take away the water burns out
until there's just a big empty space there
where all the moody stars look in on a black hole
reflecting.

DiThankyou,
Solomon's Human Lagan

P.S. LAGAN: –noun
"Anything sunk in the sea, but attached to a buoy or the like so that
it may be recovered." – Dictionary.com

This is what a crop of Lagans in Edinburgh looks like:

Leigh Adams, Andrea Gibson, Buddy Wakefield, Katie Wirsing

MY LIFE ON PURPOSE

LET IT GO

Let's let go from the get go.
Let go let God.
Let it go.
Leave it alone.
Let it pass.
Let it be.
Laissez-faire.
C'est la vie.
What's done is done.
Hang up on it.
Land the plane.
Don't get on that train.
The bus has already left.
This too shall pass.
Shake it off.
Cut your losses.
Bust loose.
Break free.
It's water under the bridge.
What comes around goes around.
Go around.
Get over it.
Get it together.
Get a grip.
Get moving.
Keep moving.
Move on.
Move forward.
Forward.
March.
Give it a rest.
Stop.
Drop it.
Squash it.
Release.
Please.

Relax.
Spilled water cannot be poured back.
Don't look back.
Enough is enough.
Stand down.
Stay still.
Be quiet.
Quit dwelling.
Yield.
Forget it.
Forgive it.
Right now.
As is.
You will be given back the years that the locusts have taken.

THE HEADLINE OF AN ARTICLE I READ WHILE PEERING OVER THE SHOULDER OF THE PERSON SITTING IN FRONT OF ME ON AN AIRPLANE

"Throw out the map and the fear, and embrace the freedom that comes from being your own best hope."

THE GOAL

Gentleman, gentlemen.

SUM CONTINUUM

Cristin O'Keefe Aptowicz told me the only harmful vestige left for me to shed is anything that is not my true instinct. My instincts tell me this is true.

AMPLIFIED STILLNESS
(START AGAIN)

I choose to end the compulsive habit of thinking and speaking insecurities. These are not my insecurities. They were habitual thoughts passed down to me. The foundation I've lain for myself is noble and true of heart and must be treated as such, with compassion and clarity.

I choose to be quiet and let forthcoming answers reveal themselves without manipulation. The hyper intellectualization, wordiness, passion and superlatives (which have often driven the engine in my ego) serve to fuel distortions of a happy life, or burn up happiness altogether. I choose to not put another log on that fire.

I choose patience under pressure.

I choose to stay present, to unlearn how to unlove,
to love, and to practice my worthiness of it.

I choose equanimity.

I breathe deep into the center of my heart.

I surround myself with friends and professionals achieving like-minded success.

I am led to consistently speak with good purpose, react as a gentleman, not instigating or projecting any foul thing, and to not internalize the negativity of others so that my presence is constantly powered by goodwill and grace. Lead me to right choices and right action, not to participate in any lies about love, and to leave helpful writing on the wall so that I might pull the next one up. Lead me to pull the next one up with real peace in my spirit, humor in my peace, and this spinal cord I bummed off a cephalopod. Jus' kiddin', cephalopods don't have spinal cords. They are bilaterally symmetrical though, and they collectively possess nearly every super power known to man, including shape-shifting, pseudo-morphing and possible teleportation.

I choose to savor this moment.

I choose ending knee-jerk reactions to that which I deem negative, including parking enforcement, cilantro and the back-up beep on commercial vehicles. For that matter, there is no need to knee-jerk-react to the positives either. Enjoying them is enough.

I choose an unassuming nature.

I choose to be held accountable.

Thank you for the vast experiences with which this life has built me.
I am thankful for what is being built.
I know it to be a fine building.
It does not stand in vain
even when it's riddled with mirrors.

Thank you for the Serenity Prayer, and the courage to follow through with right action, with listening, with learning and with stillness.

I choose to release my hope for a better past, to discontinue boasting past glories, and to not justify any poor choice with having lived a hard life.

I choose to speak with kindness and acceptance, even to myself.

I choose to be unapologetic for healthy living.

I choose to be unapologetic for living.

I choose to politely ask myself to step aside if I am in my own way.
If I do not get out of my own way, I choose to call a friend who will have me removed.

I choose to observe how I may best serve today, and then do so.
I choose to better understand service and to live less selfishly.
I choose the nature of giving not greed, stability not desperation, safe passage as opposed to craving and clinging.

I witness the gifts in the lives around me.
You really are incredible, ya know.
Good gravy just look at ya.

I choose big me big you.

I choose chin up, best foot forward, stick my landings.

I choose a safe place to land.

I choose feeding myself joy over beating myself up.

I choose not to beat myself up if I trail off course, rather, gently redirect my breath so that these standards I've accepted for myself are not buried under any unnecessary weight of any perceived shortcoming.

"I choose to not let come out of my mouth that which would contradict the blessing that is happening in my life." – Michael Bernard Beckwith

I'm giving myself a break.
Enough.
I choose to be enough.
No more ten thousand hours of more more more.
Not by force.
This work will not save me.
I release me.
Go and have some fun.
I've spent so much energy becoming better.
I choose to now live with the better, to yield to the better, to show you the better, and to let the rest unfold.
I will show up every day.
My failures have led to successes.
It is a time for practicing these successes, and for rest, and for clear reception.

I may make no decision based on panic.

Lead me away from telling lies, exaggerating truths, bragging, or manipulating people's perceptions of me. These are disservices to my practice.

I choose to breathe all known and forthcoming truths at once, deeply and consistently, inhaling and exhaling reassurance and understanding, joy and equanimity, wonderment and revelation, acceptance and integrity, commitment and flexibility, balance and ownership, staying present with the moment, observing my environment, yielding to all that is.

And when I do not do all of these things forever without fail, may I be banished to an unforgiving lake of lava shit for the devil's fat eternity.

…Or, treat myself to a good meal, some sound sleep, and another deep breath.

…Or, call Mom, tell her what's goin' on, and agree with anything she might say just to know that I have a mother.

I release my need to be right.
I know that this is the key to living life as is.
I choose as is.
Let God be God.
And let me be still
until thy will is revealed.

Nothing is against me.

THE WHOLE MONK HUNGERPUNCH

"Anyone can sympathize with the sufferings of a friend, but it requires a very fine nature to sympathize with a friend's success."
– Oscar Wilde

CONTRIBUTORS TO *MY LIFE ON PURPOSE*

- Jive Poetic stood next to me while we observed a sad and careless man at The Seattle Slam. He was making fun of Saul Williams from the stage. I motioned to raise my voice in order to shut the man down on behalf of Saul. Jive Poetic calmly reached over, put his hand on my chest and said, "Hang up on it."

- Esther Shin and I were roommates for one month of spinning planets. She was the freshest breath of air during those days. While writing "Let It Go," Esther offered for me to include the line "Spilled water cannot be poured back." It is translated directly from a Korean idiom. It is also the windpipe in that piece.

- The locust line is inspired by Joel 2:25.

- Regarding "The Goal": Jon Berardi, I aspire to cultivate your example in my own presence. Thank you for teaching me how to respond to the future. Katie Wirsing, thank you for teaching me how to respond to the past. Stephen Snook, Timmy Straw and Michael Roff, thank you for teaching me how to respond to the present. S.N. Goenka, thank you for teaching me how to not respond. To the gentlemen not mentioned at the moment, thank you for your understanding.

- Cristin O'Keefe Aptowiczh is The Wizard of Oz. She does more behind the scenes for the adult performance poetry community than most poets recognize. She sees things in big pictures. She pays big pictures forward. She points out holding patterns to air traffic control. She cares about people, and the importance of presidential trivia. If you're a writer in this community and are wondering how you got a Wikipedia page, or why anyone from Australia would be contacting you, or who wrote those reviews on Amazon, or who gave credit where it was due in the archived history of Slam, chances are Cristin had something to do with it. Without her I am not as proud to take part in our community. People have spelt her name incorrectly in nearly every publication since the day she was born. I have gone to great lengths to make sure that I correctly spell . . . Hold that thought, my roommate has toasted peanut butter sandwiches....

- Acknowledgements for "Amplified Stillness *(Start Again)*" are listed at the end of this book in order to keep things moving. They are lengthy and better suited for inclusion under *Bread*. I sure am thankful to have so many to be thankful for....

ENDLESSLY OTHER WISE

CONVERSATION WITH DANNY SHERRARD

BUDDY: Everything's impermanent.

DANNY: It would be nice, though, if there was someone to share the impermanence with.

FOR CARLEY AUCTEL'S ADMIRER

Here I sit, broken-hearted swastika,
fuck you, fuck off, fuck this,
fags burn in hell.
Jesus was a truck driver [shit smear],
died for our sins on the cross,
bore the burden is risen in the utmost
to the highest is my savior, oh Lord.
Obama Bin Laden suck Bush [dry cum drip].
Need dick, call Harold, call now for pussy.
Don't drop your toothpicks in the toilet
because the crabs will pole vault.

To bathroom stalls and dressing rooms across America:
You have not yet revealed your full potential
in the same way television has failed to show proper news,
and schools have failed to teach children from the get-go
that everything is connected,
though, I am impressed by your tendency
to accurately draw cock of various proportions.
In fact, the cock-to-vagina ratio
sketched on restroom and dressing room walls globally
is staggering to say the least.
Vaginas are just too complex, I suppose.

But on July 11, 2007, there was discovered a dinosaur language
written as clear as the air itself, flawless like a tear duct,
someone astonishing—among the graffiti swamp and fecal particulate—

had written on the men's restroom wall at the Grog Shop in Cleveland, Ohio, with red marker inside a dirty white gangland tag, the following words:

Carley Auctel,
you are beautiful
and you rock my socks
and you are perfect.

WHAT IS A GENTLEMAN?

"Someone who invests in thought before talk; an ingrained intention to treat every person and situation as if their heart depended on you. Humility, humility, levity, sincerity."
— Sarah and Forrest Middleton, my friend and her gentle husband

"A silent soldier of good will."
— Lace Williams, my cousin and friend

"A gentleman knows how to not disgrace his self or others."
— Andy Deck, my urologist and friend

"A gentleman doesn't just tolerate straight people, he accepts them."
— Paul Bennett Hirsch, my classmate and friend

"Someone who doesn't hog the free dolphin rides."
— Robbie Q. Telfer, my tour partner and friend

"I asked my friend, Aline Reynders, what a gentleman is and she said, 'My father. I don't know why but to me he will always be what a gentleman should be'."
— Matt Kouba, a gift and my friend

"Timothy Elizabeth Beezhold."
— Buddy Wakefield

A HOLE IN GOD
(FOR T.E.B.)

you appeared like a body bag
fulla hymnal books
unzipped in half I

never saw so many door jams fall
outta anyone's mouth
into math like that when

Tennessee put its crooked smile
on a wadded-up map
and sent you packin'

west

good

gospel gospel got god
stuck to the rock he made and
    and he mighta made it larger than us
    or it mighta served to save this place
sure I coulda swore I heard you callin'
for a shot at a grip on vice
    doesn't mean your mouth was moving
doesn't mean I even heard you right

all I know is that your skin keeps callin'
and I don't care if it's a busted flint
    'cause every time you pull your thumb down on it
    I get [up up] back up to my feet

again

all of them

move move
like an offering plate
on'm one by one
    it's a penchant for a savior
    a tendency to over—*run*

whatever shook do not get shook up
whatever's lost you don't get lost
    even if they say you must give more than
    everything you ever offered up

I know a voice does not come easy
I know the words fell out in bites
    I know the moment when the
abandonment looked a lot like flight
    you pulled whatever got left

inside

out right

IN LANDSCAPE
(FOR S.J.S.)

There is a chance
you will show up laughing,
made of fortified fan blades and ferris wheel lights,
true of heart and best foot forward,
our long-awaited love made easy.
Remember for sure no doubt these things:

The joy,
we are a point of complete.
This life,
standing guard over your solitude.
My eyes
are monsters for most things approaching.
I'm probably gonna need a hand with that.
This heart.
This sleeve.
Neither one of them things is all that clean.
But the rain,

my lucky number,
been doin' her part to make things right

for the light bulbs
and the bruises.
Hiding holy water was not my forte this life.
Forte
is French
for blanket fort.
I have trusted my corners to revolving doors
but am fluent in getting better.
We are fluent in bouncing back,
lifting quickly,
learning fast.

Our courage
is a natural habitat.
Ya know we're gonna build a body to keep the wolves out.
Hold my house
you humble barbarian,
this door only opens for the remarkable now.
So we will both show up remarkable.
Speak your piece from the *I can do anything*.
Say it clearly.
Follow through.

On runways.
In turbulence.
There is a book
living inside your chest
with dilated instructions
on how to make a safe landing.
It was written
for crash landers.
Thank you.
I am coming home to listen.

It is time.

Please

forgive me my distractions.
There's a freckle on your lip.
It is a national archive.
Give it to my ear
so you can see what I mean.
Here, hold my breath.
I will be right back.

There are gifts
hidden beneath these lungs.
Slide your hand over my mouth
and I will speak them.
In hang glider.
In hilltop.
From the loyalty of a landscape.
Silk in a sandpaper offering plate.
The jacket on a handsome man.
That lip
Sweet Grape, you cannibal,
kiss my eyes
until they see what it is that I wish to write down—

Your name.

Film strips of prayer.
Ribbons of a garden in stereo.
Driftwood welded to the guesthouse.
Ringfinger wrapped in a horseshoe nail.
I will meet you by the eighth day dream
in the wide open purpose of a locomotive coming
to a stand still with the sea
like thumb

on pulse

you watch

what happens

when the air

erupts

into suction cups
opening up to breathe,
like the love in my lungs
took the tip of my tongue
and finally taught it how to read,
you five-acre ladder-backed pearl book pouring
from a pileated chest of Earth.
I know our story may look like octopus ink
to the rest of the breath in this world.
Flying in under the radar,
holding to a pattern of worth,
come closer you guest of honor.
Chickens stay off the porch.

In quiet.
In kindly.
We are the house gift-wrapped in welcome mats,
your dinner's on the table in thanks of that
and the loaves of chocolate toast
and the shoreline.
In due time.
The Book of Job and of Jet Propulsion.
Rocket ships floating in a raincoat.
Playing naked checkers in bed.
It is an utterly epic arrival
every time I get to see you again.

God, *this* is what I was talking about
for like *37 years.*
A true story.
Of oceanthroat.
Of grace.
The holy goodness glory
I was praying to your face,
My Man,
this is what I meant.
And this is what I'm meant to do.
So sit me down inside us now

and let me praise the greatest good in you
by laying down my weapons,
including the shield.
In rest.
Inception.

On cue, my friend,
you came,
your name
well lit,
stenciled on the walls of Fremont County
years before we even met
in landscape,
in scope,
and so,
wing tipped,
I wrote it
down to the ground you walk on
with the heels of my helium shoes,
"Put your ear to the sky
and listen my darling,
everything whispers I love you."

ENDLESSLY OTHER WISE IN DETAIL

- Danny Sherrard was struck by lightning. After that he claims, "nothing smelled the same." This is true. Danny is the razor blade shady angels carry across the fine line. He is my friend. I am sharpened by him.

- Sarah and Forest Middleton are the parents of Mira. They speak in yeses and are conduits of clarity. When I am a guest at their dinner table, Mira leads us in a round of thanks before we eat. Everyone holds hands and speaks things they're thankful for, like goat cheese and Crayons and top hats. When everyone's had the opportunity to speak thanks, we all say, "SQUEEZE!" then we squeeze each other's hands and eat.

  In the last mile of the 30th Annual Escape From Alcatraz Triathlon, Sarah Healy-Middleton was goin' bananas for me, shoutin' out powerful reminders of who we are and why we do the things we do, but she did not lose focus on the task at hand and was well reminding me how to physically stay righted and how to show up in the home stretch. Where the course opened up near supporters and spectators, Sarah rode her bike alongside me on the grass for as long as she could. She was coachin' her heart out when I passed a man on my right who looked over at me with all his breath and said, "Where do you find friends like that?" In the moment I responded, "Well, ya can't buy'm." I sure hope my answer was good timing with regards to whatever was goin' on for him, but if anybody ever asked me again where to find friends like that I'd probably give the same answer I'd give for how to find a four-leaf clover, "You have to look." – Heidi Kunkle

- Lace Williams is my cousin. No one loves this country for the freedom it intends to represent more than my cousin does. She is the most upstanding and gracious citizen I know, and she believes in me. She paid for the production of my first CD, among a warehouse of other gifts she has bestowed upon me, including but not limited to: a sense of normalcy, backroom screenings of the big picture, and a little psychic humor. We have the same laugh, the same cheeks, and a similar drive. My journey happens in mirrors of hers.

- Andy Deck sent me a text. In it was a reference to *Outliers: The Story of Success* by Malcolm Gladwell. Basically Gladwell offers that if anyone puts 10,000 hours of time into getting better at something, they will master it. Regarding my writing, Andy wrote to me, "After all those 10,000 hours, I know you got some peace to share. Time to let the art speak beyond the cycle of redemption. Isn't that where beauty exists? Love, A.D." It's no accident that Andy introduced me to the person responsible for the poem "In Landscape." He and his partner Dave Vowels once stood up ahead and held torches for me so I could know I was moving in the right direction. No one saw them do it. I want you to know they did.

- Paul Bennett Hirsch is… okay, remember Edna Mode, the costume designer in *The Incredibles*? Paul is my Edna, only he doesn't design my clothes and he's a better listener. He makes me laugh. He's a reminder that I'm still gonna "get it" when I'm fifty. He and his partner Tim have provided eggs, and jam.

- Robbie Q. Telfer is a theme park. He once made me break character on stage and laugh till I could no longer breathe. He lives at the source of compassion and is a purveyor of truth in its abstract random forms.

- Let Matt Kouba and the whole Kouba family represent every family, friend and artist over the last ten years who have so warmly shared their homes and personal space while letting me make my way. There is not enough paper for all the thanks. Consider this proper postage.

- Timmy Straw's "Skinny Like Water" so noticeably moves me that Tim asked if I'd wanna back her up on it for an upcoming CD she's releasing. Absolutely. I've been attempting to write a worthy contribution to the song ever since. "A Hole in God" is what I will work from in the studio, and is directly inspired in rhythm and approach by "Skinny Like Water;" with slight lyric de-blockage help by Tyler Schnobelen.

- Andrea Gibson, Derrick Brown, Anis Mojgani, and I were on "The Junkyard Ghost Revival World Tour of America," 2008. We stopped in Shoshoni, Wyoming, in Fremont County, enamored by its abandoned buildings and ghost appeal. Next to a mural of Chief Washakie's head were stenciled the words, "Put your ear to the sky my darling everything whispers I love you." I got my heart set on using those words for "In Landscape," so I did. I did use it. Upon applying a search engine to them wonderful words, it appears a gentleman by the name of Jason Anderson may have written the line. It's on his album New England in a song called "Christmas." It's a good song.

"In Landscape" was written with help from and directly inspired by Stephen J. Snook.

Rilke caused the line about standing guard over solitude.

REENTRY

INTRODUCTION

"My name is Buddy. That's my real name *and* my party name."
– Derrick Brown

JOB DESCRIPTION

Show your work.

BIO

Buddy Wakefield is attempting to document the figurative contents of a man's body standing firm in the presence of all that is (and/or God). He writes poetry from the perspective of a student, tithing. His collection of tithes is filed under *Sometimes Everything* in the National Archives. The National Archives live in a building in Seattle behind barbed wire directly next door to the Center for Spiritual Living. This is true, and is no accident. Buddy Wakefield aims to cause a disarming de-haunting of accidents. There are no stunt doubles performing the accidents in his work. He works with glowing and blood. He intends to transcend trial, to craft a translation of the human spirit on a practical patch, an offering to the rips, not for filling the empty spaces; spaces are well enough empty. He is pursuing a career in judgment suspension, but sometimes he wants to blend in so badly he forgets what matters most and worries that everyone else is doing it right, or wrong. He once sat on the whole world and told it jokes about the ocean 'til everybody crumbled into tattoos of bakeries. Remember that? It was a shot at redemption. He studies propellers because they can make themselves invisible. He's collected himself enough superlatives and humongous titles to fill an oval tub with crud, but he readily acknowledges how academic poets are generally way more smart when they manipulate words and

English classes. Ghosts are haunted, not us.

GIMME YOUR SLOWEST NIGHT KITE. FILL IT WITH AN ELEPHANT ENGINE. TAKE ME HOME.

Seth Terrell.

It was the thing on my vision board I hadn't really wrapped my brain around: "Professional Gentleman." I was staring at the words and wondering what the heck I meant by that. Just then an e-mail from Seth popped up on my phone. It was a link to a video. The video was of Bill Murray in the gymnasium of his old high school talking to the graduating class about what it means to be a gentleman. This was no accident. Seth and I are happening at the same time.

Seth Terrell lives on a set-back 4-leaf-clover-filled shire in Seattle, Washington with his dog, Squid. He's 37, handsome, single and likes girls. His core is platinum, his laughter loud and welcoming, his nature that of a hippie redneck whose heart says all the right things and whose mouth releases wayward translations of said heart. Hippie rednecks are pained creatures. He is often so curmudgeonly in the mornings or after work that I want to cram a bubble gun up his nose and squeeze. On most days there is a large bowl of pudding somewhere just begging to be dumped on his head by me. I know that he at first resists life before laughing and giving himself over to his purpose, daily, but Seth ultimately embodies purpose. Anyone who's ever witnessed his power will tell you of the blinding reflection he causes. It should be noted here that people are not always blinded by light. It should also be noted that anyone who has ever lived with me at length, especially in a van, might question if I really just had the audacity to call Seth out on his morning manners… they would be wasting their time with this line of questioning; everyone knows I'm a delicate sunflower in the mornin' time. Besides, this is about Seth, A-wipe.

There is a rare processing mechanism living inside Seth's human experience, and in that mechanism is a waterfall fight. He is finding the source of his rivers and is willing to cut off the hostile branch. Seth Terrell lent me life when I had nothing left. His computer expertise has saved me thousands of dollars. He has helped me move my belongings at least five times, driven me to work when I still had day jobs, shuttled me to the airport more than airplanes, and his home has been the conduit for my creativity even more than I love peanut butter, and I can eat the pants off peanut butter. For eighteen years he's been watching me try to belong to this body, spot-checking my high ideals, and challenging my I-just-got-really-high ideals. Without him there is a completely different journey and no Buddy Wakefield as is. I'm sure the same could be said of a butterfly which flaps its wings and causes hurricanes, but no other butterfly did what Seth Terrell did. Also, he would probably prefer I use a grasshoppa metaphor over a butterfly. He likes Yoda a peculiar whole bunch too.

Seth is at the moment letting me live with him again mid-stride as I approach the next chapter in choosing my own adventure. Therefore, I am currently unable to pour pudding on his head. Instead, I shut up as often as I can remember to and observe him in this natural habitat, a series of dark caves reaching halfway 'round a warm fire, facing sunrise.

Seth, your unwavering ability to cause success is a ripple effect. You're a rock. And a star. You know these things. It will be my joy the day you are certain. I will buy front row tickets to your target practice. I will help you build the front row. I do not have any power tools because I was borrowing yours, but I will find a level and bring it.

REENTRY FOOTNOTE

- Derrick Brown is my publisher and friend and lives on a boat called "The Sea Section." I annually travel with him and Anis Mojgani on a tour we call "The Revival." I am sure of them both. They are instrumental to my fundamentals. Every year we give "The Revival Tour" a new moniker and tour America with each other. I would be remiss not to share them with you. They are essential to my gratitude.

MARCH 5, 2009
FROZEN SADDLES

Last month The Junkyard Ghost Revival met up in Fairbanks, Alaska
for one final Junkyard show.
Day of show
we made it to the dogsleds by 11 a.m.
The guide had 65 dogs.
Boy, they sure were fun and excited,
shittin' all over the place.
Just before my nose hairs froze into prisms
I could smell'm.
After my nose hairs froze into prisms
I could smell'm even more.
Cold makes a smell stick.
I learned how to harness them and guide the sled.
I also got to ride in the basket.
My guide, Leslie, guided me through
a fairly ridiculous amount of beauty.
The dogs had a blast.
Something you may not know is
dogs can poop while they're running and not miss a beat.
When the dog in the back of the pack poops
it can land dangerously close to inside the basket
and make grown men scream like baby girls.

My dogs:

My dogs:

Lunch was in front of a fireplace where we sang old
jams comin' outta the ceiling.
It was nice to get warm.

Then we headed back and got geared up for our
snow machine adventure along the Alaska Pipeline.
There were some pretty sweet jumps.
I totally caught like a foot of air.
This is Derrick explaining to me where my turbo launchers were:

After tearin' it up around the countryside
we went back to the hotel and took naps to rest up for the show that night.

It was one of our favorite times performing together.
Afterward we went to the pub on campus
where much of the audience met us for beers
and a surprise session of karaoke.
"Eye of the Tiger" pretty much got a dance crowd on the floor
and we all got to show off our eye and tiger moves.
I remember a lot of punching too.
Derrick signed up as The Gooch
and sang "My Way" by Frank Sinatra.
It was a real crowd pleaser.
One of my closer friends on this planet, Shona Strausser,
had flown in from Juneau to surprise me the night before.
It worked.
This is us dancing to Derrick's selection:

You can spot Derrick singing behind us.
He really nailed the performance:

Shona sang one last solid gold smash called "Love is a Battlefield"
while I had a simulated knife fight on the dance floor with some local ladies.
Somehow the zombies from "Thriller" got involved.
When the pub closed
we all went over to an old Fairbanks favorite called The Marlin.
There was a live band and the place was packed.
More dancing happened, and relay conversations in good spirits
and somewhere around 3 a.m. I feel like
that's when we got the bar to chant
SPRING BREAK over and over
even though it was February.
That led into us getting them to chant
U-S-A! U-S-A! U-S-A!
Man, the locals really loved chants
and banging in unison on the bar.

Back at the hotel Anis and Shona tried convincing me
that I'd eaten six ice creams from the vending machine
but I only counted five wrappers on the floor when I woke up the

next morning.

A million thanks to Caleb Kuntz and Heather Ridgway for the photos and especially to Cody Rogers for having us out.
It was one of the most fun days The Revival ever had together.

Polar,
Bare

LAND THE PLANE

GEAR UP THE BALLROOM

If anything in this book bears repeating, it is that
We're all in this together.

OPEN LETTER TO THE PEOPLE OF THE FUTURE

Before the Earth finally opened up
and swallowed its own surface
to make room for you,
The People of the Future,
there was still time enough to write this down.

By now you have found my gym bones
jammed between the door frame
crushed under my school desk,
the gum still stuck to my hair.
Yes, it was a lame place to try and hide from the end of the world.
But I am young
and passionate enough to believe
that my heroes are giving good answers.

There is no way for me to know
how many of our street signs or our libraries
you've already read,
or if you could even tell the fact from the fiction
scrawled between the lines
on our outdated text
before finding me here,
buckled like a one-way accordion,
but I will do my best to fill in the blanks
in chronological chaos.
Here goes:

We came from monkeys and tadpoles,
rainwater and clay,
accidents
and gods held together in the hallelujahs,
pulled apart like a spider web.
We were dripped down
and we were stretched thin.
I was a slide whistle in a finger trap,
but there were tricks to getting out
without making sound.

In the end
we were kids just holding our tongues,
and the whole world
lived in a land called Houston, Texas.
No. Not really.
But it sure as humid fuck felt like it.
We were stuck together
and here's the truth:

All the vampires you read about in our books
before getting to me as a detail,
those were fiction.
But the inspiration you got from our vampire songs,
that was real.
I saw it with my very own eyes.
There is a point when you should no longer watch.
I've got a hands down case against passion.
Desperate burning bloodsucker, listen carefully:

When we found the West Coast
we felt like paradise had to be more,
more than what it already was,
which was really already
quite sincerely enough.
But we couldn't fit enough in our mouths,
so most of us took to running around
breathless, and restless,
headless chickens on a mission
buying animals we could not take care of,

teaching them to depend on us
then leaving them alone.
In the future,

don't do that.
There were puppies
left alone for crates of days
and their owners had good hearts.
But even the best of us forgot how to see a thing hurting.
Even good people knew how to turn bad touch
and genocide into clichés
just to make room for more comfort.
More comfort. More comfort. My goodness. My word.
Sometimes all you will notice in my letter
is a tail
wagging when you walk in the door.

If you're reading this,
go home.
I will tell you, but you have to go home:
It was a black hole that finally ate us.
We went lookin' for it,
so it ate us.
There. Now you know.
We were swallowed by the giant gap
that got jammed between forgiveness and people.

I was learning how to close it out when you came,
inserting myself into space,
converting my mind into wine,
I was cake decorating the emptiness,
we were all rewriting sky
with fireworks
and satellites
and sugary stacks
of gun refineries
heisting the image of clouds.
We are picture games
on sunny days
for when your kid looks up at the sky now.

Get home.
Even if it feels too late.
All the dogs have survived and are waiting,
Don't chain up their love in our missing links.
Those were turned into poems on paper.
There are things we did well. Wad me up.
I will disappear in you,
forgiven in the final breath.
It all gets forgiven by each of us,
each one of us finally eaten,
each one of us finally full,
despite the incredibly nagging concern

that when you,
The People of the Future, find us here
it will be because you are digging
for something more than who you already are,
as if anything could be more.
Turn back.
Go home.
Put me and my letter and this ridiculous desk
back into the ground
with the prescriptions
and the computers
and Henry Darger's alarming heart.
Do not wake us up.
Let it rest.

Last week,
for the first time since denial,
we ceased convincing ourselves,
long enough to rest assured,
that if we finally put the practice back
into that which we know will actually work,
the West Coast might grow good enough
for everyone to walk like paradise
and quench this barking thirst,
our boot straps pulled up out from under
the weight of the world we paved

all the way back to the start of New York
with all the words that we just didn't mean,
words we didn't even believe every day,
poor goddamn people on the T.V.
hating everything
in an effort to feel important.
I was clearly *very*
very important.

When I say *I*
I usually mean *we*.
We
pushed cigarettes into our face,
then with the other hand
danced around the edge of this place
to look worthy of making a statement,
or to keep us from feeling alone.

And that worked.
Until it didn't.

The consequences are immediate,
so when you clap
ya might try to free both hands up
if ya ever really wanna act to close out the gap
we have grown between forgiveness and people.
Let that honest head of yours
have a snowball's chance to climb
back down
through your throat
and into your body
so it can see
the miracle you came here to be,
and just how good you look
when you're not compared to anything.

I
I looked good in these shoes and a swagger talk.
I learned to walk well in these words is all,
even when they're hard to read,

dirty and dug from the ground.
At least I spoke directly to ya,
because your timing is perfect
and your weather is perfect
and because I knew that you,
The People of the Future, would dig for me here.
Even the Earth when she eats us
has her soft spots.

BREAD

- This book was formatted in a way that allowed me to write with gratitude and credit due. It is for the folks who walked (or ran) with me to this point. If you're reading from a distance and we're meeting for the first time, welcome. I hope it was a fine way of getting to know each other.

- Many of the notes to myself in "Amplified Stillness *(Start Again)*" were highly inspired by the following folks with whom I've had the honor of sharing life. Some of their words, concepts, and surgical maneuvers are simply being passed forward, though I have used my own interpretation to make it happen. Any direct quotes are noted. That being said, due and thorough thanks for guidance into healthy thoughts/feelings/actions respectfully go out (some repeatedly) to S.N. Goenka, Reverend Michael Bernard Beckwith, Reverend Kathianne Lewis, Tara Brach, Tresa B. Olsen, Lace Williams, Remond Liesting, Steven Arrowood, Reinhold Niebuhr (Serenity Prayer), Danielle Plunkett (for being the catalyst of the title of this book, for reminding me to lay down the shield, and for your unwavering grace), Sarah Healy-Middleton (for Nora B), Nora B (for teaching me to speak my name to its face), Hugh Prather (as ever), The Tamblyn Family (for the space to cultivate a better man), Tiffany Hill, Jon Berardi, Marc Kelly Smith (for "Pull the Next One Up"), Brian Crooks (for the Center for Spiritual Living), Perry Sjogren, Jeffrey Olsen (my brother; for giving me *The Four Agreements*), Curt Tomashoff (for saying "thoughts lead to feelings lead to actions;" sometimes it just takes a friend to state the obvious), Mike Roff (for Niagara Falls, dancing drunk on life through the park, the freezing bath, the hot air balloon ride, and for letting it go in perfect form), Andy Deck and Dave Vowels, Anis Mojgani (for the note in my wallet, to open only in case of an emergency), Ross Szabo and Heidi Pendergast, Barb Rowan, Daemond Arrindel, Emily Wells, Keeli Shaw, Meredith Masters, Vicki Robinson, Sandy Beasley (my sister and friend), Beau Sia, Derek and Karen McGhee, Cristin O'Keefe Aptowicz, Karen Finneyfrock and Lane Stroud (both, for stepping into the ring and distracting the ref so I could beat the ten count), Andrea Gibson (for "Thank Goodness"), Derrick Brown (for "Church of the Broken Axe Handle"), Oliver Klomp (for remembering to remember), Ani DiFranco (for the company of lead dancers), Todd Sickafoose (for your voice of reason, and echoing National Monument), Andy Borger, Mike Dillon, watching twelve seasons of *The Ultimate Fighter* (with respect to Jonathan Brookins), life with/without Quantum Learning Networks, and Stephen Snook (for running interference and finding me again, for a safe place to land, and for reminding me that anything is possible).

- Thank you to Joel Chmara, Shannon Magnuson, Anis Mojgani, Robbie Q. Telfer and especially Tim Stafford and Dan Sullivan for the inspiration to instigate chanting *SPRING BREAK* in the middle of a bar in Alaska in February.

- Thank you Mindy Nettifee for your book, *Sleepyhead Assassins*. It taught me how to relax my language just a little bit more on the page.

- Thank you Jonathan Drew Plunkett for being twenty-months-old once and wanting a frozen yogurt stick from the freezer. I thought you wanted alphabet magnets off the surface. You threw them on the ground and groaned, so I thought to open the fridge for you. You shut it and cried a little, so I opened the freezer for you and pointed to the wrong food. You screamed *"NO!"* with such frustration I did not expect you to calm down for quite some time. I pointed to the frozen yogurt stick and you clapped and it was over. Thank you for teaching me that my anger is rooted in not being received according to my intention, or when my communication is limited, or when someone tries to sell me on nearly anything but frozen yogurt sticks [or peanut butter]. It's a very upsetting thing indeed to keep company with people who do not understand what I'm saying. Or why. Or when I do not have the words to say them.

- Thanks quite much to The National's "Vanderlyle Crybaby Geeks" for helping me finish this book.

- With special thanks to my spiritual leaders S.N. Goenka, Tara Brach, Reverend Kathianne Lewis and Reverend Michael Bernard Beckwith who are each responsible for verbalizing a great deal of the self discovery and acceptance I'm experiencing. Views and quotations from their works and discourses have highly influenced the notes and poems herein throughout.

- After we finished playing a soccer game, Malcolm Smith asked whether or not I was drinking alcohol these days. He was trying to find out if I wanted to go for beers. I searched for the answer and its qualifications and thought to justify a thing or two while I fumbled for words (I hadn't been drinking the year prior) when Malcolm said, "Budford, it's a yes-or-no question. Land the plane."

ANOTHER CONVERSATION WITH TODD SICKAFOOSE

BUDDY: No staring.

TODD: I'll stop staring when you no longer look like a child.

NEW WRITE BLOODY BOOKS FOR 2011

DEAR FUTURE BOYFRIEND
A Write Bloody reissue of Cristin O'Keefe Aptowicz's first book of poetry

HOT TEEN SLUT
A Write Bloody reissue of Cristin O'Keefe Aptowicz's second book of poetry
about her time writing for porn

WORKING CLASS REPRESENT
A Write Bloody reissue of Cristin O'Keefe Aptowicz's third book of poetry

OH, TERRIBLE YOUTH
A Write Bloody reissue of Cristin O'Keefe Aptowicz's fourth book of poetry
about her terrible youth

38 BAR BLUES
A collection of poems by C.R .Avery

WORKIN' MIME TO FIVE
Humor by Derrick Brown

REASONS TO LEAVE THE SLAUGHTER
New poems by Ben Clark

YESTERDAY WON'T GOODBYE
New poems by Brian Ellis

WRITE ABOUT AN EMPTY BIRDCAGE
New poems by Elaina M. Ellis

THESE ARE THE BREAKS
New prose by Idris Goodwin

BRING DOWN THE CHANDELIERS
New poems by Tara Hardy

THE FEATHER ROOM
New poems by Anis Mojgani

LOVE IN A TIME OF ROBOT APOCALYPSE
New poems by David Perez

THE NEW CLEAN
New poems by Jon Sands

THE UNDISPUTED GREATEST WRITER OF ALL TIME
New poems by Beau Sia

SUNSET AT THE TEMPLE OF OLIVES
New poems by Paul Suntup

GENTLEMAN PRACTICE
New work by Buddy Wakefield

HOW TO SEDUCE A WHITE BOY IN TEN EASY STEPS
New poems by Laura Yes Yes

OTHER WRITE BLOODY BOOKS (2003 - 2010)

STEVE ABEE, GREAT BALLS OF FLOWERS (2009)
New poems by Steve Abee

EVERYTHING IS EVERYTHING (2010)
New poems by Cristin O'Keefe Aptowicz

CATACOMB CONFETTI (2010)
New poems by Josh Boyd

BORN IN THE YEAR OF THE BUTTERFLY KNIFE (2004)
Poetry collection (1994-2004) by Derrick Brown

I LOVE YOU IS BACK (2006)
Poetry compilation (2004-2006) by Derrick Brown

SCANDALABRA (2009)
New poetry compilation by Derrick Brown

DON'T SMELL THE FLOSS (2009)
New Short Fiction Pieces By Matty Byloos

THE BONES BELOW (2010)
New poems by Sierra DeMulder

THE CONSTANT VELOCITY OF TRAINS (2008)
New poems by Lea C. Deschenes

HEAVY LEAD BIRDSONG (2008)
New poems by Ryler Dustin

UNCONTROLLED EXPERIMENTS IN FREEDOM (2008)
New poems by Brian Ellis

CEREMONY FOR THE CHOKING GHOST (2010)
New poems by Karen Finneyfrock

POLE DANCING TO GOSPEL HYMNS (2008)
Poems by Andrea Gibson

CITY OF INSOMNIA (2008)
New poems by Victor D. Infante

THE LAST TIME AS WE ARE (2009)
New poems by Taylor Mali

IN SEARCH OF MIDNIGHT: THE MIKE MCGEE HANDBOOK OF AWESOME (2009)
New poems by Mike McGee

OVER THE ANVIL WE STRETCH (2008)
New poems by Anis Mojgani

ANIMAL BALLISTICS (2009)
New poems by Sarah Morgan

NO MORE POEMS ABOUT THE MOON (2008)
NON-Moon poems by Michael Roberts

MILES OF HALLELUJAH (2010)
New poems by Rob "Ratpack Slim" Sturma

SPIKING THE SUCKER PUNCH (2009)
New poems by Robbie Q. Telfer

RACING HUMMINGBIRDS (2010)
New poems by Jeanann Verlee

LIVE FOR A LIVING (2007)
New poems by Buddy Wakefield

WRITE BLOODY ANTHOLOGIES

THE ELEPHANT ENGINE HIGH DIVE REVIVAL (2009)
Poetry by Buddy Wakefield, Derrick Brown,
Anis Mojgani, Shira Erlichman and many more!

THE GOOD THINGS ABOUT AMERICA (2009)
An illustrated, un-cynical look at our American Landscape. Various authors.
Edited by Kevin Staniec and Derrick Brown

JUNKYARD GHOST REVIVAL (2008)
Poetry by Andrea Gibson, Buddy Wakefield, Anis Mojgani,
Derrick Brown, Robbie Q, Sonya Renee and Cristin O'Keefe Aptowicz

THE LAST AMERICAN VALENTINE:
ILLUSTRATED POEMS TO SEDUCE AND DESTROY (2008)
24 authors, 12 illustrators team up for a collection of non-sappy love poetry.
Edited by Derrick Brown

LEARN THEN BURN (2010)
Anthology of poems for the classroom. Edited by Tim Stafford and Derrick Brown.

LEARN THEN BURN TEACHER'S MANUAL (2010)
Companion volume to the *Learn Then Burn* anthology. Includes lesson plans and worksheets for educators.
Edited by Tim Stafford and Molly Meacham.

WWW.WRITEBLOODY.COM

WRITEBLOODY
QUALITY AMERICAN BOOKS

PULL YOUR BOOKS UP BY THEIR BOOTSTRAPS

Write Bloody Publishing distributes and promotes great books of fiction, poetry and art every year. We are an independent press dedicated to quality literature and book design, with an office in Long Beach, CA.

Our employees are authors and artists so we call ourselves a family. Our design team comes from all over America: modern painters, photographers and rock album designers create book covers we're proud to be judged by.

We publish and promote 8-12 tour-savvy authors per year. We are grass-roots, D.I.Y., bootstrap believers. Pull up a good book and join the family. Support independent authors, artists and presses.

Visit us online:
WRITEBLOODY.COM

CPSIA information can be obtained at www.ICGtesting.com
Printed in the USA
LVOW11s1156171213

365587LV00003B/15/P